Training The Prophets

Dr. Margaret Wright

TRAINING THE PROPHETS

All rights reserved. No part of this publication may be reproduced, stored in a retrieval system, or transmitted, in any form or by any means, electronic, mechanical, photocopying, recording, or otherwise, without the written prior permission of the author.

©Copyright 2008 Dr. Margaret Wright, Lees Summit, MO 64064

Unless otherwise indicated, all Scripture quotations are taken from the King James Version of the Bible.

Scripture quotations marked AMP are taken from the Amplified Bible AMP. The Amplified Bible, Old Testament copyright ©1965, 1987 by the Zondervan Corporation. The Amplified New Testament, copyright ©1954, 1958, 1987 by the Lockman Foundation. Used by permission.

Please note, Eagles Eye Press LLC, Inc. publishing style capitalizes certain pronouns in Scripture that refer to the Father, Son, and Holy Spirit, and may differ from some Bible publishers' style.

ISBN No. 9780615528076

PUBLISHED BY EAGLES EYE PRESS LLC
119 SW ROSE GARDEN LN
LEES SUMMIT, MO 64064
WWW.EEPKC.COM

TRAINING THE PROPHETS

THIS BOOK IS DEDICATED TO...

This book is dedicated to Bishop (Dr.) Daniel M. Jordan and Pastor Irma Keith (deceased). I watched their lives up close and personal as well as from a distance. Their tutelage has been invaluable in my development. I cannot begin to imagine the shipwreck my ministry would be in right now had it not been for their vision to see in me what I did not see in myself. I implore everyone in ministry especially Prophets to seek out good mentors.

Thank you Bishop Jordan

Thank you Mother Keith (posthumously)

TRAINING THE PROPHETS

TRAINING THE PROPHETS

DEDICATION POEM – A HOLY WOMAN

God sent this woman from the heaven's above
To speak the Word and give kind love.

She was the most powerful woman of them all
No devil or evil spirit can make her fall

She has been chosen to train the others - the Prophets
But the devil came to her and told her to STOP IT!

She prayed and spoke the word of Jesus
Then said Devil you cannot come between us

The holy woman walked through the land
Grabbing the people by the hand

There they go singing the gospel songs and praising the Lord

TRAINING THE PROPHETS

And the holy woman goes on her way speaking the word
It was now their turn to go their way
They have so much to accomplish that they had to pray

The holy woman was pleased with her qualities
Her and God are one in UNITY

****

I dedicate this poem to my loving Grandma that has made so much of an impact on people's lives including mine. I wish her good success with her new book and hope people learn a lot from it because this woman is powerful in the Lord. I love my Grandma with all my heart. She is my angel that flows with me.

Morgan Joyner-Ford (Granddaughter - age 16)
Los Angeles, California

TRAINING THE PROPHETS

TABLE OF CONTENTS

	Dedication	3
	Dedication Poem	5
	Introduction	9
	Foreword	13
	Acknowledgement	17
1	Components of the Call	19
2	Etiquette	39
3	Proper Discharge of Duties	55
4	Are You Willing to Pay the Price	71
5	The Human Side	81
6	The Prophet as Student	95
7	The Prophet and the Supernatural	107
8	Humility	119

TRAINING THE PROPHETS

TABLE OF CONTENTS

9	Samuel's Posture	*125*
10	Summary	*131*
	Call to all Prophets	*143*
	Prayer of Salvation	*147*
	Author's Biography	*149*
	Appendix A - recommended reading list	*153*
	How to purchase products	*155*
	Other Products	*156*

TRAINING THE PROPHETS

INTRODUCTION

I was awakened from a serene sleep by a powerful yet calming voice gently speaking my name. **"Margaret"** is all He said. I got out of bed to search for the origin of the voice – determined to explore every area of the two-bedroom apartment I shared with my young child. I looked in my daughter's room but all I heard was the steady breathing of a child in a not-a-care-in-the world slumber. "I must be hearing things" I thought so I retired back to my bed. Again, the voice said **"Margaret"**. OK, now I am getting a bit concerned. Is someone in the apartment beside the two of us? Another search resulted in finding nothing. "So maybe I will **not** go back to bed" I thought. There is something really strange going on. I decided to call my spiritual mentor Evangelist Irma Keith (who would later accept the call to Shepherd God's people). I explained to her

TRAINING THE PROPHETS

the two occurrences of hearing my name called and my subsequent search which provided no answers. She gave me these instructions: Read *1 Samuel Chapter 3*. God is calling you as he called Samuel. Follow Samuel's pattern and answer God as Samuel did.

Sure enough – God called my name again. With a trembling and uncertain voice I answered the Lord with – "Speak Lord thy servant hears". God then said, "You shall be my mouthpiece, my teacher, and my scribe." Thus in the summer of 1979, I began my call to the ministry as Prophet, Teacher, Scribe. I learned so much from my mentors Pastor Irma Keith and Bishop Daniel M. Jordan. Invaluable lessons that I want to share with other Prophets. God has inspired me – YES – commanded me to write this book. He has kept the scripture *Acts 8:30-31* (In which the Ethiopian eunuch states that he cannot understand the scripture unless someone guides him) branded in my mind saying "G*uide*

TRAINING THE PROPHETS

the prophets". "Teach them what I and your mentors have taught you." He states that "some are in error and some simply do not know how to operate in the prophetic call."

So, I am writing this book. It is my prayer that you will be **Enlightened, Encouraged,** and **Empowered** to stand in the Prophetic call God requires of you!

I am here to serve. I am here to serve God. I am here to serve His creation – mankind. I am here to serve.

Serving Him with Joy,
Prophet Margaret C. Wright

TRAINING THE PROPHETS

FOREWORD

It is a great joy and honor to address those that read, purchase, or recommend this great book of "*Training the Prophets*". Dr. Margaret Wright is a capable, able, and seasoned woman of God. Being under my leadership as her pastor for 20 years has caused her to be an effective and worthy woman of God. Seeing her grow by leaps and bounds unto a spiritual giant has caused me to rejoice. In spite of all her hardships, struggles, and disappointments, she has become an astounding specimen in the Lord's army.

My desire for you is this, let not the wisdom found in this book fall on deaf ears or on an unteachable or rebellious heart. I have been a servant of the Lord for 60 years in the ministry and yet going strong and am grateful to endorse this book *"Training the Prophets"*. Some of you may not have met Dr. Wright or even unfortunately may never meet her, as we have not met Elijah (in the Old Testament who had the school of the Prophets) or even the privilege of meeting the 12 apostles (as they walked with Jesus in the flesh over hills and mountains); but, thanks be to God for the anointed pen from her hands on such an awesome printed page of literature which can be transmitted and planted into your heart as well as your ministry.

Every born again believer has a ministry but everyone does not have the office of a Prophet. Absorbing every word from her biblical heart of God's word comes not to hinder or to hurt you but to help you. You may get a "new" revelation jumping from the pages of this book through the Holy Spirit that (1) you are not a prophet that others or you have said you were, (2) you are not ready to be a prophet according to God's providence before you were even born, or (3) is confirmation from God bearing witness that you are walking in the vocation wherein you were called *(Ephesians 4:1 KJV)*.

Such truth in this publication will blow your mind in avoiding a waste of time, unfounded claims, and ignorance. Again it can help those that are true prophets to stay on course, improve and perfect the principles that are ready to die *(Revelation 3:2 KJV)*.

This book is far past due for this 21st century revelation of God's principles. Revelation cannot be **_taught_**, it must be **_caught_**. Catch this through prayer and fasting as you digest these precious truths that you will not be ignorant of Satan's devices *(2 Corinthians 2:11 KJV)*.

HUMBLY SUBMITTED BY,
BISHOP DANIEL M. JORDAN DD., TH.D, PH.D
PRESIDING PRELATE, SENIOR PASTOR, AND FOUNDER
THE PENTECOSTAL CHURCH OF GOD IN CHRIST
MIRACLE REVIVAL FELLOWSHIP
6300 SWOPE PARKWAY
KANSAS CITY, MISSOURI 64132

ACKNOWLEDGEMENT

I thank my Lord and Savior Jesus Christ for the inspiration, information, instructions, and insight provided to me by the Holy Spirit which made this book possible.

I acknowledge and thank my wonderful husband Pastor Carlton F. Wright (Senior Pastor of Christ Is The Answer Ministries, Inc) for being so patient during the long nights I spent at the computer. It is so important to have spousal support as you take on a project of this magnitude. He has ALWAYS been my biggest fan. He believes that I am called to the prophetic ministry and encourages me to pursue God's instructions with gusto. Thank you so much Mr. Wright!

I thank my family for being so supportive during this journey.

TRAINING THE PROPHETS

I thank the Christ Is the Answer Ministries congregation. You support me. You pray for me. You encourage me. You monetarily bless me. You are indeed great examples of "Saints" of God.

I thank Dr. Zalmer Nichols – Chancellor of Faith Bible College – Independence, MO for the liberty you extended to me to allow me to teach the Prophets a more excellent way – God's way.

I thank each student that attended the "Training the Prophets" class. It was truly an honor to share with you what God had given me.

Thank you so much Dr. Jacquie Hadnot. Your expertise in making this book into a reality truly "blows my mind". You are my sister in the Lord and such an inspiration of what God can do if we just stretch outside of our comfort zone.

I thank those friends that critiqued and edited the book - Prophet Cecilia Clark, Prophet Lois Sheppard-

TRAINING THE PROPHETS

Haynes, Prophet Sandra Martinez, and Prophet Alonda McGowan.

Please keep me in your prayers?

TRAINING THE PROPHETS

TRAINING THE PROPHETS

CHAPTER 1 – COMPONENTS OF THE CALL

What an exciting journey we are launching. In this chapter we will explore the mechanics, (if you will), of effectively functioning in the realm of the prophetic. Immediately a question should come to mind – "What exactly is my call"? "Am I called to the ministry of a **Prophet** or is the **Gift of Prophecy** operating in my life? Is there really a distinct difference between the two? The answer is a definite – YES!

1 Samuel Chapter 3 recounts the events of the direct call from God to Samuel regarding his life-long ministry. God's instructions to Samuel were extremely detailed and took a certain kind of "ear" to hear with clarity. Remember that *1 Samuel 3:7* states that *"Now Samuel did not yet know the LORD neither was the word of the LORD yet revealed unto him"*. Yet with his very first encounter with God, Samuel hears with profound precision and obeys faithfully. This is indeed the emerging components of a Prophet.

You will find that every once in a while I may take a "rabbit trail" diversion. So when you see the "baby rabbits" you will know that the Spirit of God has given me some really good information to impart to you and I need to tell you while it is fresh on my mind. I promise to always let you know about these excursions as it happens so that no one gets lost along the way. Oh, by the way, I believe both men and women are called to the ministry (office) of a Prophet. Galatians 3:28 – "There is neither Jew nor Greek, there is neither bond nor free, there is neither male nor female: for ye are all one in Christ Jesus." I really hope I have not lost an audience with that statement. If you are not convinced now – keep reading and I know that the knowledge that the Spirit releases in this book will assist in changing your mind.

Back to the components...

You see the prophet at any given time will use several of the gifts of the Spirit to perform his/her duties. Yes, the prophet will employ the Word of Wisdom and the Word of Knowledge simultaneously. He/she may be moving in the gifts of healing and miracles at the very same time and so on with all nine Gifts of the Spirit. One of the components of the Prophetic ministry is that the prophet routinely operates in at least two of the gifts of the Spirit at any given time; thus, the distinction from the person that has an "anointing" in the Gift of Prophecy. He/she does not flow in other gifts on any regular basis because remember their "anointing" resides in the operation of the Gift of Prophecy.

TRAINING THE PROPHETS

Component 1. The Prophet utilizes at least two gifts of the Spirit at any given time to dispense His duties as prescribed by the Holy Spirit.

A true Prophet of God hits the target each time. By this I mean that there should not be a statement that he/she is "accurate 75% of the time". Is God only correct 75% of the time? What nonsense. Oh you say "Who is that exact"? I say a Prophet that has stayed before God in prayer and supplication; has a <u>lifestyle</u> of immediate obedience to the Spirit of God; and, has cultivated the art of "hearing" God. Now **that** person is correct each time he/she says…"The Spirit of God is saying"… If Samuel had that testimony in [1 *Samuel 3:19 – "And Samuel grew, and the LORD was with him, and did let none of his words fall to the ground"]*, then we know that it is possible for all Prophets to have that same testimony. End of discussion!

TRAINING THE PROPHETS

Look at this. 1 Samuel 3:1 – "And the child Samuel ministered unto the LORD before Eli. And the word of the LORD was <u>precious in those days;</u> there was no open vision ". We as Prophet should have a love for truth and a burning desire to deliver a PURE word. The Word should be so precious that we are compelled to get it right. We are in the midst of a dry land, hungry for the unadulterated word of God. It is our duty to supply NOTHING short of accuracy.

Component 2: The Prophet is exact in his/her regurgitation of God's message. Psychics are 80%, 75%, and 65% accurate. Not the REAL Prophets of God Almighty (*El-Shaddai*).

TRAINING THE PROPHETS

Moving on...

The Prophet will experience what I call the *progressive* anointing. This will manifest itself in visions & dreams; hearing God's audible voice; seeing, hearing and being ministered to by angels; physical manifestations e.g. I get "goose pimples" when a divine, profound truth is spoken to me by the Spirit of God or in conversation with others. *Numbers 12:6* makes an emphatic statement that God will make Himself known to the prophet, that is, speak to him through visions and dreams. Samuel was called to the ministry by God's audible voice. In the passage of scripture *2 Kings 6:8-23*, Elisha the prophet is accompanied by the heavenly host as his military guard and protector. He sees the angels and prays that God will allow his servant to see them as well.

If we would research the entire 66 books of the Bible, we will see a common thread throughout the

TRAINING THE PROPHETS

Word depicting the holy alliance of angels with the Prophets of God. As the Prophet develops into the "mature" instrument God predestined, we will see this progressive anointing in action. Elisha went from student to mentor and from there to teacher of many. We see a continual increase in the anointing evidenced by the steady increase in power of his words and miracles done through him by God.

I want us to note something extremely important in 2 Kings 2:1-15. Elijah is about to leave the scene and Elisha has been his constant companion. The prophets in Bethel, Jericho, and Jordan recognized that the mantle of Elijah was transferred to Elisha. There was no competition between them. **None**! They acknowledged and respected the anointing upon him. How wonderful it will be when we the Community of Prophets will value and accept the unique anointing

TRAINING THE PROPHETS

upon each of God's Prophets and not look upon one another as "competition". God is using all of us in His Kingdom work. Let's come together as a cohesive group united in our efforts to get the Word of God delivered to all mankind. The complexion of this <u>Community of Prophets</u> is slowly changing to this. Pray that individually we will commit to making this end-time vision a reality.

And you too, Prophet of God, will experience that progressive anointing. Do not get in a hurry to do everything at once. All through the Bible we see the development of men and women from novice to mature instruments fit for God's use. We need not be mature in the things of the Spirit before God uses us, yet God is requiring growth so that we can provide a more excellent presentation of who God is and what He has mandated for man to do.

TRAINING THE PROPHETS

One of the best examples of this is the Saul-to-Paul saga. Even in Saul, overnight going from persecuting the saints to preaching the Gospel, we see God using him mightily in the synagogues. As Paul, he becomes one of the most illustrious prophets of the New Testament churches. God knows what is in you and He will take advantage of all that He has put in you just as soon as you make yourself available to Him.

Allow God to "grow" you and remember He is a God of time and seasons. Elisha may have wanted that double portion sooner than it was delivered to him but he realized that he had to wait until God's time. God has a time for you. He will open doors for you. He will elevate you. He will use you in the way that best suits the kingdom work. Move with His flow. Do not be swayed by what others do in the Prophetic. <u>*You will make a shipwreck if you try to mimic it.*</u> You must be compliant with the anointing God has put in you, not what you saw someone else do.

Component 3. The progressive anointing is a very necessary pilgrimage that each Prophet must travel. How we start out on this prophetic road cannot be how we finish. We must advance, cultivate, and become seasoned in this CALL – but in God's own time!

God is holding the Prophet accountable in this call. God trusts you with His words - Speak when God says to speak. There is life and death in what you say – Hear what the Father says RIGHT (i.e. accurately) the first time! OBEY! OBEY! OBEY

King Balak of Moab sent for the prophet Balaam because as he stated in *Number 22:6*, whom Balaam blessed was blessed and whom he cursed were cursed. Why? Balaam had that kind of power with God. Strictly

TRAINING THE PROPHETS

because he was a prophet of God, a fringe benefit is God honoring what the prophet says.

Still skeptical? Look at *2 Kings 2:22-24*, Elisha cursed the children that mocked him and God honored that word in a decisive and final way. Saul (aka Paul) cursed the false prophet in *Acts 13:4-12* which resulted in the conversion of the deputy of that territory. A Prophet must take extra care with the words he/she uses – in all circumstances. Our words carry "**weight**" with God. Don't forget also, that God is holding us accountable for the "motives" that accompany our words. Who gets the glory out of it – God or Satan?

*Also note something. As God exposes us to the world, others will know that the prophetic anointing is upon us. Do we have to announce this to everybody? NO. WE DO NOT! Put **your arrogance** in check. Spend* *extra care reading more about this in Chapter 8 on HUMILITY!*

This story of Balaam is an excellent teaching tool. It covers the spectrum of all the good things a prophet should do and bad things he/she should never do. We have give Balaam such a bad reputation. But if we are honest with ourselves, we see some of Balaam characteristics in our ministry.

So, you don't think you have any of Balaam's "genes" in you? Well, let's take a better look and you decide for yourself. He heard God and was "going" to obey. What stopped him? Self and greed. He must have thought "Perhaps God would change his mind if I keep asking for clarity" or asking "God what do you "really" want me to do?" <u>Be careful that your quest for clarity does not turn into a refusal to do what you heard God say the **FIRST TIME**.</u>

NOW THAT WAS A POWERFUL REVELATION!

Component 4. The Prophet has a responsibility that goes along with the call. Say <u>only</u> what God says. <u>Obey</u> every instruction He gives you and do it <u>right</u>!

We must discuss the idea of aloneness vs. loneliness. Much of what God shows us is for us to know but cannot share with others. To stay true to this aspect of the call will require much fasting and staying before God. Some things are for you to know and pray about – period. We have got to be careful that we do not get hung-up in the **"I told you that was going to happen"** spirit; or, in the **"I need to tell someone so that they will know how powerful I am"** spirit. Everything God shows you is not necessarily meant to happen. Christ has given us power to bind those things that are authored by the devil – in your life and others as well.

TRAINING THE PROPHETS

I am not stating that the prophet should not have friends but I am saying that our lifestyle is a bit different from others. God will make some unusual demands upon us and we must be very discriminating in selecting those with whom we confide. THIS IS NOT A LONELY LIFE BUT IT DOES HAVE PERIODS OF ALONENESS. God has designed our lives this way.

Why aloneness? Our best example is our Lord Jesus. He spent many hours alone with God. He received some divine communications that He could not share with the disciples. The Prophetic office is not a dripping faucet of "God said" or "God told me". Please do not compromise the call by having diarrhea of the mouth. Many times God is telling you not to say anything. Please yield to the Spirit and keep your lips closed during those times. Let me help you right here. THE ONLY WONDER IS JESUS THE CHRIST – not you or I.

Component 5. We must be comfortable with ourselves and our call because we are going to spend a lot of time alone. Everything God tells us is not for public consumption so learn to discern between what is and what is not.

Validation absolutely needs to be mentioned here. I have heard so many prophets say "What if people don't believe in me?" My response to that is - a prophet is without honor in his own home and own country *(Matt 13:57)*.

Jesus has prepared us for rejection and for those that do not believe in our ministry. Those familiar with His life in his hometown were offended that He was presented as a Prophet and Messiah. Their unbelief in Him being sent by God caused the power of God to be diminished. Who was the loser – not Jesus? That community did not get the healing and deliverance that was as close to them as touching the hem of Jesus' garment.

TRAINING THE PROPHETS

So, do not look for validation from family, friends, or those close to you. For that matter, do not look for validation from anyone other than God. He called you and will equip you. The question really is – DO YOU BELIEVE IN YOURSELF AND WHAT GOD HAS MANDATED FOR YOU TO DO.

Listen – be very careful who you get yourself entangled with as your go on the quest for validation. Watch your associations. What you will find are some folks in ministry looking for a man/woman in ministry that is known for integrity and good stewardship. So they want to be "hooked-up" with you to add validation to the "madness-and-mess they're trying to "pull" on God's people. They may build-up your ego. IT IS ALL A TRICK OF THE ENEMY! Do not be deceived. Your reputation is on the line. You are an *instrument and representative of El Chay (The Living God). Wait on God.*

In *Acts 13:42-52*, Paul and Barnabas had an experience similar to what Jesus experienced and found that their ministry was not accepted by the Jews. They were not dissuaded by this – Oh no. They continued vehemently and souls were converted. Many times your response to rejection must mirror that of Paul and Barnabas – shake the dust and move on to a people that will believe in you and what God is doing through you.

Component 6: The Prophet has no time for wallowing in a pool of pity because some will not believe in his/her ministry. For everyone that will not believe in you, God has dozens that will and that need you RIGHT now! So, get on with kingdom work and seize every opportunity to work for Him that sent you.

TRAINING THE PROPHETS

Other questions arise as you move along this Prophetic path. I am a female. I'm married. I have commitments to my husband and children. Can I really give my "ALL" to the ministry? I am a man with great responsibility already. How do I juggle home, work, spouse and this calling to?

Again, the word of God has our answer. Let's delicately approach this matter. First, examine your "hearing". What is God saying? That command will line up with scripture. If we have responsibilities at home, believe me, God will not have you all over the world ministering to everyone and leave your home in disarray.

What did the prophets in the Bible do? Deborah presented herself as a wise woman yielding to authority whenever required but taking the lead only when necessary. Jesus' family was in ministry with him – His earthly half-brothers and of course His mother, Mary.

TRAINING THE PROPHETS

Do not exclude your family but include them in this journey that you have embarked on with the Lord.

Always understand your place. Being a prophet of God does not give us a license to do whatever we want in the name of "I'm just obeying God". God's order is this – Him first, spouse, family, career, etc. Your <u>first</u> ministry is to those at home.

God is a God of order so allow me to reiterate – ORDER BEFORE THE ANOINTING. The Spirit is NEVER out of synch with God and His will. Everything happens for the Prophet within a unique phenomenon called God's timetable. Minister to those God brings in your "space" and allow yourself to grow from there. You can do it – juggle all these things in life. God would not have called you if He thought you could not perform your duties.

Component 7. Make time for God and family. This is very important. God cannot and will not use men/women that are out of order. Get your house in order before you embark on a prophetic work for God. If you have a spouse, remember as one-flesh, you both have a vested interest in doing this right. Let your spouse and family know what God is doing and saying so that they will be prepared for satanic attacks. Oh yes – there will be many.

♡ **What's on my heart:** Proverbs 14:12 informs us that every person has a way that seems right but it will only end up in disaster. Doing things your way is not how to live a life as a Prophet and be successful at it. You must get all your instructions from God. Those instructions can be through a Mentor, Pastor, etc. but it must be God's way. Understand the gifts of the Spirit because they are your tools. Stay in God's presence so that you can fine-tune your hearing and obedience. Allow God to elevate you and always walk in integrity. Cherish those times of isolation with God because that is when divine revelation flows freely. Lastly, believe in yourself and know that God called you for this time and season.

TRAINING THE PROPHETS

CHAPTER 2 – ETIQUETTE – THE DO'S AND DON'TS

We absolutely are responsible for our actions as prophets. God is holding us accountable and the blood of souls we have hindered will be on our hand. For this purpose, it is so important for us to address Prophetic Etiquette. So many "anointed" prophets do not know how to conduct himself/herself in this great call God has commissioned them to fulfill. The anointing does not give us a "license" to do and say whatever and whenever we feel the "unction of the Holy Ghost". Am I saying disobey God, of course not?

What I am saying is that like any other gift, skill, or ability, we must be trained. Paul even instructed Timothy to **"study"**. The problem is that this ministry like most things in life requires hard work. God trains us in many ways. He will allow you to make a "good" or "bad" choice and suffer the consequence of that choice. God is merciful. He will give you instructions but again, the final decision to obey lies with us. Part of our discussion in this chapter will delve into all the "do's" and "don'ts" of actual ministering. It's so very true that many people have walked in the call for years and do not know the "etiquette" that should be adhered to in the prophetic call.

Decency and in order

Many churches do not recognize the ministry of the prophets because the leaders (Pastors) have seen too much "abuse of power" syndrome. The prophet speaks for God, and he/she cannot speak anytime they want. **THIS IS NOT A FREE FOR ALL.**

We must exercise our gifts in a decent and orderly manner. When preaching is going forth (i.e. fishing for souls) that is not the time to have a corporate "word". You may have a private "word" – but if it does not relate to salvation – write it down and give it to the individual later. When a minister is spiritually fishing it is no different than natural fishing. There must be a certain atmosphere to catch fish. Fish, like souls, do not want to be caught – the least disturbance and they are lost.

Confusion is a great distraction to fishing. On the shoreline the fishermen cannot be confused about what to do and how to do it. They will catch nothing; likewise, the prophet should not interfere while the minister is trying to catch fish. The fish (soul) will be distracted and be lost.

God indeed gives the prophet a "word" – no doubt about it. It may relate to the fishing for souls. So what do you do? One of the best things to do is pray that God either gives the minister that is going forth the message or that God will open a door for you to deliver the

TRAINING THE PROPHETS

message. Oftentimes, we do not pray that the minister gets the word. WHY? We want to deliver it ourselves. It is an act of growth and maturity when you do not get the "credit". Pray that the minister of the hour gets the "word from the Lord". Remember the most important thing is that the "soul" gets the message – is that not true? God should get the glory not us.

*What a great responsibility the Prophet has. Satan would love to make us a spectacle to bring shame on ourselves and God. Resist the temptation to be seen and heard. You will have your time and season sooner than you think. Live by this principle at all cost – **ORDER BEFORE THE ANOINTING!***

So what about those times when others are ministering like in a one-on-one prayer line? Again that is not the time for you to "give a word" to those in line. Allow the Lord to use the minister of the hour. If the person has neither the prophetic call nor the gift of prophecy, he/she will be told by the Holy Ghost that there is a "word from the Lord". I have seen this happen many times and the prophet in the audience came forward and delivers the "word". It's all really about God and Him ministering to the souls and not at all about us. Always have pen & paper with you just for times like these. You can jot down the "word" from the Lord and give it to the individual later. These are practices that I have adopted that work. Not only is it confusing when a prophet decides to give out "words" to those in the prayer line but it is also disrespectful to the minister of the hour. In essence the prophet is saying "God is talking to me not you". Is that cruel or what? Can you visualize two singers singing different songs at the same time – two builders building two different style houses on the same foundation – that is confusion!

See *Amos 3:3*.

What about those times when someone gives a personal prophecy and the prophet has additional information for the recipient? What do I do? If this happens during one-on-one ministering, again, write it down and give to the individual later. If it happens during what I call "free time" (before/or/after church, parking lot, grocery store, library), after the other conversation is finished, then by all means deliver the "word". Be careful to state that you have an **additional** "word" from God which complements (harmonizes, goes with, accompanies, or supplements) what God has already spoken to the individual. This is EXTREMELY important. Watch this scenario:

> Person gets a "word".
>
> You overhear it
>
> God gives you a "word"

TRAINING THE PROPHETS

Be very careful not to give the attitude or any appearance that the original "word" was not true and that you are coming to "refute" the original "word". That will cause the recipient to think that the "word" from the other person was not true.

But suppose the prophecy WAS NOT TRUE? God told you – THIS IS NOT TRUE! What do you do now? Remember, the bible says *1 Chronicles 16:22 "Saying, Touch not mine anointed, and do my prophets no harm"*. Denouncing the prophetic words of another prophet or person with the gift of prophecy is very tricky. This is a time to be like what *"Matthew 10:16 calls wise as serpents, and harmless as doves."* This situation must be approached with wisdom and humility so as not to destroy the soul that was ministered to. Humble so as not to destroy the ministry of the one that did the ministering. So what do you do? Again, we are talking about one-on-one ministry. Try to talk to the one that

TRAINING THE PROPHETS

GAVE the "word", and then tell him/her what God has given you. Do not take an attitude of rebuke but in an "I'm sharing the word with you that God gave me" type attitude. Ask them what they think about it?

Now, one of two things will happen. They will say, "Yes, I can see what God is saying. Did you tell the person – or maybe YOU SHOULD GO TELL THEM WHAT GOD TOLD YOU – it will really bless them." **Or** you may get the other reaction – "and so" attitude. **Or**, the "What do you want me to do about it" attitude. **Or**, "I did get that from the Lord". **Or**, "I said what God told me" – defensive attitude. At that point – BACK OFF. If you can find the person, deliver the "word" in a way that states emphatically GOD TOLD ME TO TELL YOU THIS. Allow the individual "to discern" which is true, or if God leads you – state that you are concerned about the "word" you received and that "God told you "to make sure they had THIS "word" as well.

TRAINING THE PROPHETS

If the person makes statements like "Was that a false word?" "Are they a false prophet?" "I don't want to receive their "word" anymore." Truly, truly be lead by God if you are forced to take this path. *Be very careful how you proceed – many souls are at stake – a minister's reputation is at stake.* Matt 7:15-23 gives us a picture of Christ denouncing them in the day that we all stand before God. At that time, Christ is the author of the rebuke. He refutes that lie! Yet God says in *Matthew 24:11, "And many false prophets shall rise, and shall deceive many. For there shall arise false Christs, and false prophets, and shall shew great signs and wonders; insomuch that, if it were possible, they shall deceive the very elect."* Why not simply state that the real proof is in the fruit – does that "word" come to pass? Does it produce "Godly" results? Is God glorified in it? Did God himself honor the "word" by making it true? Remember, we are trying to preserve souls not destroy them.

TRAINING THE PROPHETS

All through the Bible God reveals to us we will encounter false prophets. God (Himself) will deal with the false prophet. We must simply conduct an experiment as stated so eloquently in *1 John 4:1-6*. Our job is to prayerfully and boldly (with compassion) expose the truth. Try the spirit. Let that person know that the spirit of truth and the spirit of error are in the land. Don't leave them confused! Let them know that ultimately God is the judge and we can only inspect FRUIT!!!

What about a corporate prophecy that is false? How do you handle that? First, look at *1 Cor 14:27-33*. There should be no more than 3 tongues & interpretations (corporately) in one service. Note that Paul did not say that there should not be any more than three prophecies, meaning that there can be more than three personal word prophecies. However, delivering a corporate prophecy (tongues and interpretation) is out of order when the Speaker of the hour has started his/her message. So the Lord has put a limit on that type of corporate "interruptions". The bible states in *1 Cor 14:29 "Let the others judge".* Who are the "others"? The "others" are the prophets that are present. If we do not have the specific "word" believe me - we (as prophets) do have a "prophetic feeling" for the "truth or false" of what is said. Listen carefully to the Holy Spirit regarding your next actions. God may tell you to speak with the Pastor regarding the word but you must be receptive to that leader's response whether it is positive or negative. Understand that you may not have the opportunity to correct every false prophecy.

Hear me clearly – If you are not the leader of the gathering (Pastor, asst. Pastor, president etc.) or have not been expressly given permission by the leadership – DO NOT OPENLY REBUKE A CORPORATE PROPHECY – THIS IS NOT YOUR JOB. If God wants you to do this, the Holy

Ghost will OPEN a door – I say the HOLY GHOST will open a door – NOT YOU to refute the prophecy. Do not go in and destroy another man's/woman's church by being OUT OF ORDER!

Delivering a message to another Prophet

It is difficult to "speak forth" to another prophet what God has given you. It is sad but the "pride" that resides in a prophet makes it difficult for him/her to "receive" from other prophets. *1 Cor 13:9 "For we know in part, and we prophesy in part."* This statement written by Paul reveals to us that God only gives us "A PART" a portion (if you will) of revelation. We may not know that God has already revealed that and more to the Prophet (recipient) and God has a chosen path the recipient must take. A negative response may be elicited. Remember that the prophet is not held accountable for the response and actions of the people to whom he/she

TRAINING THE PROPHETS

has delivered the message. No, the prophet's requirement is to deliver.

If you were Agabus delivering this message to Paul (*read Acts 21:10*) and you got the response that Paul gave him, how would you feel? Would you think that Paul doubted your word? Would you immediately start to defend yourself and your call? No, you are not responsible for the outcome. We must remember that God has a plan for us all and sometimes the prophetic voice of God is just "confirmation" of what MUST take place. The prophet that receives the word is responsible for what he/she does with that information.

God may give you a "word" for another Prophet. Do not feel inadequate or fearful. Deliver only what God said and no more. Set your face as a flint (*Isaiah 50:7*) and you will not be made ashamed.

In the Old Testament, the elder prophets trained the younger prophets. They "sat at their feet" to learn.

TRAINING THE PROPHETS

This is still true today and we have that added benefit of the Holy Spirit training us.

God expects the church to accept, care for, and assist in the maturity of the prophet. The prophet is a great help to the Pastor – saying those hard, harsh, often revealing words that God sends to correct, uplift and expose so that the body of Christ is strengthened.

God hides the prophet for a time – just as He hid Moses, Jesus, etc., so that the prophet is not discovered too soon before his/her time of release into the prophetic ministry. The church should be on alert and ready to protect that budding prophet.

A prophet may have many, many, harsh tests where humility and dependence is concerned. This is necessary so that he/she learns that the ONLY SOURCE FOR THEM IS GOD, NEVER HIS/HER OWN POWER, KNOWLEDGE OR RESOURCES. *Phil 3:3* tells us to have "NO CONFIDENCE IN FLESH" – note even our own flesh.

TRAINING THE PROPHETS

Every GREAT (or what man calls great) prophet has had some terrible trials in his/her life. Humility is one key to success in this call and God will get it from the prophet at all cost. Humility brings about complete and total obedience.

The Prophet must learn how to hear God speaking in dreams and visions; fine-tune his gifts of perception and knowledge by practice; combine bold forthrightness and reserved courtesy. He must know the law (the word) and when and how to follow the Spirit beyond the letter of the law in mercy. He must learn the power and ways of intercession and how to call the body to it. The prophet is not sent to "create" more prophets that are his/her own mirrored image. NO! The prophet is sent to develop the body so that the reflected image is that of the spotless bride. The bride (body of Christ) must find herself and not merely be a copy or shadow of the prophet.

TRAINING THE PROPHETS

The prophet is an enabler. He/she wants to move the church into a pursuit of perfection and maturity for this is the will of God. Today's prophet is interested in you getting your heart right – then you WILL obey the Law (word of God). The prophet can never set himself apart from man as if he/she has been made perfect. Remember Paul's words – "1 Tim 1:15 *"This is a faithful saying, and worthy of all acceptation, that Christ Jesus came into the world to save sinners; of whom I am chief."* At that time, Paul's handkerchiefs and aprons were healing the sick but Paul always remembered His source and his frailties as a mortal being. Please be aware of gimmicks, tricks, shows and show-casing your skills!

TRAINING THE PROPHETS

♥ **What's on my heart:** It is all about God and not all about you. Souls are at stake. That should be our motivation for all that we do. God is holding us responsible for "how" we administer our call and gifting. Jesus had compassion even when he was delivering harsh words. We are not GOD – just instruments of God. Our charge is to "SERVE". God gets the glory and credit – ALWAYS! You will be sought out. No need to make yourself known by being out of order so that you may be **seen** and **recognized**.

The church should not be a stifling atmosphere, which will hinder the growth and maturity of the prophet. Many would-be prophets have been damaged by the church; growth stunted; disgusted; shut down; discouraged; disconnected; rejected; despised; ran out of the church; and, not allowed to grow.

Knowing all this, we still say YES TO THE CALL TO BE A PROPHET. Amen!

TRAINING THE PROPHETS

CHAPTER 3 – PROPER DISCHARGE OF DUTIES

Perhaps some of you are asking the same question I posed to my mentors. "I have accepted the call but what do I do now?" What are the mechanics of this call? The information that follows is just a few key elements of the proper discharge of our duties as Prophets. Use this as a springboard to discover more of what God requires of you in this critical hour of Christian history.

How is the Truth presented?

The whole truth and nothing but the truth. <u>At All Costs</u>. <u>At All Times</u>. <u>Under All Circumstances</u>! (To thine own self be true. To God be true. To God's creation (Mankind) be true. Too many people believe what you say). We must be accountable for what we say and HOW we say what ... *THUS SAITH THE LORD.* It is imperative that we expound the truth while preserving the soul. By that I mean that we must consider the person. The level of maturity of the soul should dictate how we impart the truth to our audience. Too many souls have been damaged by a word from a Prophet. *John 16:13* declares to us that the Spirit of Truth will speak for God. We should rely totally on the Holy Spirit (our partner in ministry) for our information. He will not lead us into error. He will speak only what He has heard from the Father. Would the Father ever be wrong? I think not. The Holy Spirit will also tell you **how** to say what needs to be said. We should consider the temperature/climate of our audience. The truth may have to be fed to them as a mother feeds an infant his/her nourishment. Can they digest strong meat? No, not at this time. Can they feed themselves? No not yet. Do we mask the truth – no not that either. What we must do is deliver the word in a way that the soul will

TRAINING THE PROPHETS

not be crushed and back away from God. A fine line to walk – yes it is. Only with the guidance of the Holy Spirit will you succeed in this.

There are times when a harsh truth must be delivered. As Prophets this situation comes with the territory. We cannot back away and ask God to choose someone else to do it. Remember the fruit of the Spirit. Everything must be done in love, joy, peace, longsuffering, gentleness, goodness, faith, meekness, and temperance. We must love mankind so fervently that we will say whatever needs to be said to preserve man's spiritual and natural life. Just because the word is hard or harsh does not mean we have to deliver the message with an attitude of hardness or cruelty. God gave Ezekiel some harsh words to deliver to Israel as recorded in chapter 33. He did not rebel or shirk his duties. HE SAID WHAT GOD TOLD HIM TO SAY.

TRAINING THE PROPHETS

As we rebuke, we are held accountable for how it is done. When Nathan was sent to King David (1 Sam 12), do you not suppose that he had some reservations initially about rebuking the King. Yet he went and cleverly approached King David in a way that the king had to accept the word from God. **PROPHETS, BE VERY CAREFUL WHAT YOU SAY TO GOD'S PEOPLE.**

I PLEAD WITH YOU!

We are in the Ministry of "RECOVERY".

We are trying to save lives. We are here to short-circuit Satan's plan. Keep your emotions out of the picture. Harness your prejudices and put all partiality under the blood. God will show us some very evil and compromising circumstances of his people. We cannot allow what we know about them to cause us to like, dislike, or feel disgust toward them. Our job is to deliver the message – end of story. Our methods may not always be understood. We will be judged by other Prophets and people in general. You may be the only person that understands how and why God told you to minister in that manner.

A prophet must have the gift of discernment.

It is his/her greatest asset. Discernment will help us not judge another prophet's ministry on face value but will allow us to see the move of God in His unique use of that Prophet's "style". We must not compare their delivery with our own. God uses each of us as it pleases Him and not according to our desires. Of course, discernment will allow us to know when it is God and when it is not. Then, wait for the Holy Spirit to instruct you in how to use that information.

You MUST have the anointing.

The Holy Ghost ALONE knows the fullness of God

(thought, mind, will, purpose). He MUST be IN CHARGE! *Rev 19:10 - AMP* - Jesus is the all in all of prophecy. Anointing is needed for exactness or clarity. We can only get that with the face-to-face encounters with God. *Deut 34:10*...a place of "open-heaven".

End-time Prophets Either Restore or Destroy.

As we rebuke, we are held accountable for how it is done. In the story about Elisha and the taunting children, we find that Elisha (*2 Kings 2:23-25*) cursed the boys in the name of the Lord. He was not responsible for how God would deal with them. He most probably did not see the she-bears destroy the children. He only knew that God and God's man were being disrespected and mocked. As we read further in this book, we do not find anywhere that God rebuked or chastised Elisha for his actions. I would infer that God saw nothing wrong with how this was handled.

TRAINING THE PROPHETS

We can then say that we must not "say" out of our emotions but, only repeat what you hear from the Holy Spirit. Take the story found in *Acts 5:1-11*. Ananias and Sapphira had devised an evil and greedy plot to deceive the men of God. If Peter had been angry and struck out at them (knowing what the Spirit had shown him), then the wrath of God would had been on him as well as that couple. Peter gave the couple many opportunities to repent and change their stories. Peter did not call death upon them. Sapphira could have repented and told the truth and not had to face the same plight as her husband. It was their choice to lie instead. Remember God does not violate our "free will". We continue to develop our craft by the constant consumption of the Word and fervent prayer in the Holy Spirit. These two elements will ensure that we are hearing from God; that we will yield to the correction of the Holy Spirit; and, that we will be scripturally accurate when we deliver a "word from the Lord". If we do not maintain this posture, we will be those prophets that destroy and not restore.

I cannot emphasize enough the importance of face time before God. A prophet's *proper* posture must be on his/her knees or prone before God. We must be people of prayer, so that our clarity stays <u>crisp</u> and <u>on-target</u>. The prophet is shown so many things not to tell but to commit to intercessory prayer. There will be times when what the prophet has prayed against has saved lives but no one will ever know. God gets the glory and the prophet's work *seemingly* goes unnoticed. Such is the life of the New Testament – end time prophet. If you are interested in getting credit and notoriety, you are in for a *RUDE* awakening.

We may "see or know" something but God may not want to change it but prepare us for it. We are then to pray and prepare ourselves anyway we can. Suppose

TRAINING THE PROPHETS

Christ had decided to heed what the disciples said or saw or what maybe he saw in a vision regarding his demise. Would we be saved today? If Paul had heeded Agabus regarding his imprisonment and death, we would not have the book of Romans today. If you recall Jonah got mad when the people of Nineveh repented and God spared them.

Does the prophet always get it right – absolutely not! If they were absolutely correct all the time, who would the people follow – the prophet or God? Perfection is only found in Jesus; thus, the reason we as prophets are only the "mouthpiece" of God. He is the source. We do not know anything unless God shows us or tells us. In *2 Corinthians 4:7,* the statement is made that we are "*earthen vessels*". We are flawed and not fit for use until God shapes us into a vessel worthy for his service.

TRAINING THE PROPHETS

The prophet cannot say…"It's just what God said." "Take it up with him if you don't agree. " **If a prophet were in error in the Old Testament days (*Deut 13:5*) he was put to death.** In the New Testament days, God deals with him as well as with the recipient with grace and mercy.

The prophet's call is to address God's people first and foremost…usually not the general public. *Matt 7:6* "*Give not that which is holy unto the dogs, neither cast ye your pearls before swine, lest they trample them under their feet, and turn again and rend you.*" The prophet must give his warnings to the RIGHT people. If it is to a whole congregation, make sure everyone hears it from the prophet. Receiving the wrong warning is very dangerous. When a prophet has a message for a specific group tell only that group and make sure they know it is for them only.

TRAINING THE PROPHETS

God does not want a prophet to fold up because he failed, but to let the lesson of it be scored deeply into his heart. Don't take yourself too seriously. Laugh at yourself. We don't go through our prophetic life making one mistake after another but we must realize that God's grace is extended to the prophet as well.

Prophets are often right in the middle of a mess (not of their own doing, I might add). The mess does not consume him. He can relax in the mess. He can make sense of the mess.

The hireling prophet

Balaam was a freelance sorcerer – a hireling prophet. He cursed or blessed for monetary gain. *Number 22:6b-7* states in the NIV – *"...For I know that those you bless are blessed and those you curse or cursed. The elders of Moab and Midian left, taking with them the fee for divination."* Ungers dictionary defines divination as the pagan counterpart of prophecy. Demonic spirits inspires divination and the Holy Ghost inspires prophecy. The prophet of the true and living God is the only authorized medium of supernatural revelation, according to God's word <u>seeking knowledge of the future and future events</u> is an insult to our God. Romans 11:29 states in the Amplified version – *"For God's gifts and His call are irrevocable. {He never withdraws them when once they are given, and He does not change His mind about those to whom He gives His grace or to whom He sends His call.}"* Balaam was used by God but was not "right" himself.

Balaam inquired of God but would use and listen to "other" gods or sources. Balaam had a reputation for getting the job done but for a **price**. In *Numbers 22:12*, God told Balaam not to curse the Nation of Israel because they were blessed; but, Balaam was driven by greed, and inquired repeatedly of God hoping that God

TRAINING THE PROPHETS

would allow him to fulfill what was needed to get the promised bounty. This proves two things. Balaam did not "know" God. Had he known God He would know that God never changes. Secondarily, Balaam was not accustom to obeying God. Here's a question: **IF GOD CHANGED HIS MIND AND TOLD BALAAM TO GO WITH THE MEN, WHY DID GOD GET MAD WHEN BALAAM WENT?** Did God change His mind and release Balaam to go though He first told Balaam not to go? In *Num 22:19*, which states – *"Now stay here tonight as the others did, and I will find out what else the LORD will tell me."* (Why ask God again? He heard clearly the first time. I believe Balaam wanted the riches that he could get if he cursed Israel.) *Numbers 22:20* states *"That night God came to Balaam and said, "Since these men have come to summon you, go with them, but do only what I tell you."* (In this situation, what would you have done? God told you not to go and now He is telling you to go?)

TRAINING THE PROPHETS

Numbers 22:22 reads this way – *"But God was very angry when he went, and the angel of the LORD stood in the road to oppose him".* (Clearly God did not expect Balaam to go.)

When we are out of step (tune) with God, our anointing is severely hampered. Why did Balaam not see what a mire donkey could see in the spirit? Why? Balaam was operating in self and out of greed. Why did not Balaam think it strange that his donkey spoke to him? Was this a commonplace act or was Balaam so far into self that he ignored the supernatural implications of God having to make a donkey speak to get his attention.

Balaam (which was not walking in purity and truth) did not have the "spiritual eye" and therefore could not "see" the angel as he stood in the roadway. God had to open Balaam's spiritual eyes.

TRAINING THE PROPHETS

A true Prophet of God

We must say what God says, whether we like it or not. In *1 Kings 17:1 – (AMP version)*, it states – *"ELIJAH THE Tishbite, of the temporary residents of Gilead, said to Ahab, As the Lord, the God of Israel, lives, before Whom I stand, there shall not be dew or rain these years but according to My word."* (God then told Elijah where to go because of the lack of rain. Not before the curse of no rain but after.) In *1 Kings 18:1 – (AMP version)*, we find these words *"AFTER MANY days, the word of the Lord came to Elijah in the third year, saying, Go, show yourself to Ahab, and I will send rain upon the earth.* (Honoring Elijah's word – God sent rain at the appointed time.)

True and false prophets have discovered how to get God's attention. Balaam knew how to entreat God *(Numbers 23:1-3)*. Peter had to give an account to the apostles in Jerusalem because the Holy Ghost had fallen on Gentiles (*Acts 11:15-17*). The same thing happens to Balaam. He wants the money and he wants to curse Israel but he cannot withstand the power of God. In the midst of Balaam's second oracle (blessing of Israel), we find him compelled to state the true nature of God. This is found in the NIV translation of *Numbers 23:19* (which believers quote frequently) – *"God is not a man, that he should lie, nor a son of man, that he should change his mind. Does he speak and then not act? Does he promise and not fulfill? "*

In verse 20 of that same scripture, Balaam is not completely disobedient. He recognizes God's authority and obeys his words. We had better be careful what we say *"in God's stead"*. Do we want to be cursing God's anointed or blessing God's enemy? We can see from verse 27-30, that Balaam did not learn his lesson. Why is he entertaining cursing Israel at all? God has already told him what to do.

TRAINING THE PROPHETS

The spirit of God **did** come on Balaam. God can use whom He chooses. Balaam did not curse Israel but he did advise the King Balak in how to tempt Israel into disobeying God. See *Revelation 2:14*. The men of Israel were enticed by the women of Moab to engage in sexual immorality and to worship and sacrifice to Moab's pagan gods. For this God caused a plagued that took 24,000 in death. Israel repented. Balaam was killed in a battle between Israel and the Midianites (*Numbers 31:8*). Such is the tragic but all too common end to the hireling (false) prophet.

♡ What's on my heart: *Ephesians 4:11-14 (Amp & Message translations)* tells us that our jobs as prophets is to: prepare God's people for works of service; fully equip the saints to do the work of ministering toward building up Christ's body – the church; help the saints reach unity and maturity – fully to develop within and without. God needs the prophets in this critical hour as spiritual Paul Reveres riding through the territories sounding the alarm not that the British are coming but that **Jesus is coming – GET READY!**

TRAINING THE PROPHETS

CHAPTER 4 – ARE YOU WILLING TO PAY THE PRICE

The Prophetic call has some severe sacrifices attached to it. Many prophets, in lieu of making the necessary sacrifices, have embraced a life of luxury and fulfillment. God warns that the false prophet will make merchandise of his people *(2 Peter 2:1-3)*. These prophets are purely after "gain". But you, prophet of God, are you ready to "give-up" whatever, to heed the call that God has upon you? Are you ready to experience the hurt, ridicule, shame, or dangers that await a prophet of God that will tell the truth under ALL circumstances? Before you answer resoundingly, **YES**, let's explore what some Prophets have to tell us about the life that is totally sold out, dedicated, and devoted to the Prophetic Call!

ELIJAH AND BAAL'S CREW *(1 Kings 18:16-40)*. Elijah had to be certain that he heard from God because he was about to embark on a life-threatening mission. God instructed Elijah to "challenge" the prophets of Baal. This was a "put your money where your mouth is" situation. He had better be clear in his mind of what God's instructions are and totally confident in the "power" that God had entrusted to him. Elijah also had to be secure in his walk with God and in his influence with God as well. If he ever needed God to back him up – he needed it now!

Elijah also knew that his only support would be from God. The people had wholly embraced the ways of Baal-the false god. Elijah dare not think that he had anyone praying for him (though he may have had a remnant). He knew that there could be no open support for him from the people. He knew that what he did, he did alone.

TRAINING THE PROPHETS

Just a note. Elijah did such great exploits that day. But in the very next chapter (19) we see him running from one little woman – Jezebel. Why? As Prophets, we must search ourselves to see if there are any "Jezebels" in our lives. What I mean is that we must determine if there are people or situations that cause fear in us – fear to be a **prophet**. We need to **confront** it and <u>GET DELIVERANCE FROM IT</u>.

Back to the fearless Elijah!

Elijah was not afraid of an audience. He told Ahab to gather the people so that they could witness what God was about to do. We may stand alone. We may be among those that do not believe in our calling but as surely as God moved for Elijah, He will move the same way for today's end-time prophet. Was Elijah selling <u>"wolf tickets"</u> – definitely HE WAS!

TRAINING THE PROPHETS

I was reminded of this scripture when I read the number of Baal's prophets. God's math is very different than ours. Why do we care how many false prophets oppose us? We have God and His heavenly Host backing us up. We can be as bold as Elijah to call them out and say – "You try your god and I will try mine".

Be neither surprised nor distracted by whoever it is that Satan may use to challenge you. Ahab was Elijah's "kinsmen" and king. Yet in *1 Kings 21:20*, Ahab calls Elijah his "enemy". We cannot allow family, friends, spouse, or anyone to dissuade us from taking a stance against confronting and **challenging** those who would question the validity of who you serve and the call that is upon you. Be prepared for harsh words from those close to you and even those in the church. ARE YOU WILLING TO PAY THE PRICE?

The audience will play a "wait" and see who wins" game. They may be "lukewarm" – singing your praise of

TRAINING THE PROPHETS

how anointed you are and then on the next hand saying "I'm not sure God even called them". STAND FIRM. BE OF GOOD COURAGE. DO EXACTLY WHAT GOD INSTRUCTED YOU TO.

Know What You Are Doing. Elijah spoke only what God gave him to speak to the people. He knew that it would "incite" the prophets to really go to any lengths to prove him wrong. Know what you are doing and what you are saying and be prepared for the consequences of what you say. Can you imagine if Elijah did not have a consistent life of fasting, praying and staying before God? Do you think he would have been successful in defeating Baal's prophets? You can "*boast*" in God when you know your relationship is sound with God; when you know that God will do exactly for you what he says He will; when you have experienced the power of God; when you have sought him in secret, He will reward you openly.

TRAINING THE PROPHETS

1 Corinthians 1:27 lets us know that we will be used by God to do those things that may seem unusual or downright silly. Like Elijah, we must obey and allow the power of God to move. We cannot question the validity of what God wants to do through us. Logic and intellect must give way to the "RAW" power of God. Elijah's story exemplifies the point that it is imperative to **"hear right"** what God will say. We must get the specifics and not move before God's time.

The prophet must remain in control of the situation. Elijah imposed upon the prophets of Baal God's instructions for the test of power. We cannot back down from Satan. Tell him what you and God are going to do. Instill fear in him and his "boys"! Maintain the atmosphere that you want. Don't give Satan an opportunity to change the atmosphere. Make Satan realize that he is on "our turf". The prophet must **STAY IN CONTROL.**

TRAINING THE PROPHETS

Elijah told the prophets in essence "GIVE IT YOUR BEST SHOT". Allow Satan to make a joke of himself. Let him brag, yell, do whatever he thinks he needs to do. Don't be caught off guard by his actions. The devil is a trickster and will try to show you up. Remember, you are the "voice of TRUTH". You have the "right" answer. You "speak" in God's stead.

Stay cool and calm. Give Satan whatever time he needs because in the end, truth will WIN. Do not be weary in well doing. So, it takes a while to "prove" that you are truly a prophet of God. So what? As long as you do what God has said, in His own time, He will expose you to all as the TRUE VOICE OF GOD – THE TRUE PROPHET.

Enjoy making a complete monkey of Satan. Keep your sense of humor. Don't be so rigid and so serious all the time. You do not have to prove yourself ...do you? You should know who you are. So, laugh at the little challenges Satan sends your way to try to disprove your Call. God will always win.

Beat Satan at his own game. Elijah used the same methods that Satan used but who emerged the victor? Elijah did! Don't let Satan off easy. Elijah slew the prophets of Baal. He had no mercy on them. We cannot afford to have mercy on Satan. We must utterly destroy his false words, false actions, and false power. The people must see that God will not tolerate evil in any form. We must call evil out for what it is and utterly destroy it in the lives of God's people. If we let them off then we do them a disservice. I know that we are dealing with souls but again I say" WE CANNOT ALLOW EVIL TO EXIST IN ANY FORM. THE SOUL IS TOO VALUABLE TO ALLOW SATAN TO HAVE ANY CORNER OF IT. Yes – use wisdom. Yes – use discretion. Yes – use compassion on the person but SHOW NO MERCY TO SATAN – **NONE!**

TRAINING THE PROPHETS

Your mind will be attacked. A "lying spirit" has been unleashed and is going forth to "discredit" the truthful prophet of God. That spirit has been put into the mouths of some prophets so that the world (both body of Christ and secular) will make the assumption that all present-day prophets are false. It is most interesting to see how the lying spirit affects the prophet. Look at the state of mind of Elijah, you, me or any prophet. A prophet cannot afford to be confident in himself. A prophet cannot afford to expect the "same" anointing to work each time. A prophet cannot afford to think of himself as "super Prophet" – nothing touches me. I am invincible! A prophet cannot afford to forget – though he may stand physically alone – that he has supernatural power at his verbal command and with him at all times.

Elijah's mind played games with him *(1 Kings 19)*. Elijah experienced fear. Elijah experienced panic.

TRAINING THE PROPHETS

Elijah experienced thoughts of suicide. Elijah experienced pride. Elijah experienced a feeling of being all alone. Elijah experienced God in a new way. Elijah experienced humility.

Elisha has a different account *(2 Kings 6)*. He was confident. The other prophets panicked. Elisha was viewed by other prophets as superior. Elisha took all limits off of God and what God could do through him (Elisha). Elisha was accurate in his instructions to the King. Elisha was confident that he heard from God. Elisha was known to his enemies to be a "true" prophet of God. Elisha saw in the spirit. Elisha knew the power of God. Elisha showed no fear. Elisha had power with God to ask the impossible of Him. Elisha bestowed compassion upon his enemies. Elisha turned an enemy into a peaceful neighbor that respected him.

TRAINING THE PROPHETS

What's on my heart: I would be remiss if I told you that the cost for this call was minimal. God will ask you to give-up everything so that He can replace it with His tools and attributes required for the ministry. *Luke 14:28* reminds us to "count up the cost" and I am asking that you perform that exercise so that you are fully persuaded in your own mind that you are **"ready"** to accept and complete this prophetic assignment – for life.

TRAINING THE PROPHETS

TRAINING THE PROPHETS

CHAPTER 5 - THE HUMAN SIDE

As Prophets we have personal struggles. We are human beings. We are not perfect people. We cannot allow others to put us in the category of perfection because we cannot abide there, that place is reserved for Christ. The prophet (like the other members of the five-fold ministry) has unique personal struggles that must be addressed. Our discussion today will center on many of those struggles, what the word says about it, and how we are to cope with or defeat those very struggles Satan will use to deter, deflect, and defeat us.

There should be no competition or competitive spirit within this call. God has preordained a specific job for each prophet to do. Each prophet has a specialty and must allow God to fine-tune that specialty. John the Baptist wrote no books nor performed any great miracles yet Jesus stated John was great. We cannot afford to compare our ministry and gifts with any other.

TRAINING THE PROPHETS

God made us different so that each of us could reach those persons our difference would attract.

Inadequacy is a constant battle. Satan may pose these questions to you. "Are you really ready for this?" "God, you are taking me too fast?" "God, you are taking me too slow." "Are the people ready for ME!" DO NOT ALLOW THIS DEMONIC SPIRIT TO MAGNIFY YOUR SHORTCOMINGS. You will grow in this call. **I KNOW YOU WILL!**

Suspicion is always lurking about. Satan is an accuser of the brethren. He will accuse you to your face. These are the things we say. "Other prophets as well as others in ministry are against me." "The people do not understand the anointing that is upon me." "I am forced to be alone." "I cannot tell anyone how I feel or what I am going through." "If people see the human side of me they will no longer believe in my ministry." These are all statements planted by the enemy. **DO NOT BELIEVE ANY OF IT!**

TRAINING THE PROPHETS

Self-criticism is one of the worst satanic attacks we will encounter. "Was that word really from the Lord or was it me?" "Did the Pastor accept me as a prophet?" "Is God pleased with me?" "I can deliver that message anytime; does it need to be now?" "They" will not receive what God says "from me". "I'm too young and not mature enough." "I've served my time and should just let the young people go forth."

If everything I have mentioned thus far has not been an issue for you, then continue to read. Satan will physically attack you. If Satan cannot stop the prophet any other way, he will SEVERELY attack the body. The prophet must know when it is time to rest and get away from ministering. The prophet needs intercessors that will pray because there may be times the prophet CANNOT pray. The prophet is not superhuman – the body is susceptible to common ailments. The prophet must recognize when it is a common sickness, satanic attack on the body, or a "thorn in the flesh".

There are many aspects to consider as we take the helm of the prophetic vessel – "the call to the prophetic ministry". **The enemy comes to DISCREDIT the prophet! Understand that this is Satan's ultimate goal.** God is moving the prophet into the realm of precision. It is OK to desire to be used by God. We must still be quiet until or if He speaks. Who does the prophet have an umbilical cord attachment to? Is it a prophet in the bible or in our lives? Why does the prophet feel that kinship? Only you can answer the question as to whether this is a *godly* alliance. What similarity of anointing that is upon you, is similar to another prophet's anointing and why? If the prophet has a kinship with the anointing that is upon another prophet, I submit **that** the prophet needs to do further exploration into that ministry. The prophet needs to explore **that** individual's struggles. The prophet needs to explore how God deals with **that** individual. God may deal with you the same way. The prophet needs to explore the administration of the anointing in **that** individual because it may be very similar to his/her anointing. Prophets have all had Jonah experiences. We have not always done exactly what God wanted at the exact second He wanted it. Do not fall into a trap – God never has to do the same thing twice. He has a wealth of methods at His disposal. He instructed Moses to do something different in providing water for the children of Israel but Moses was comfortable doing it the same *old* way. Hear God and obey!

WAIT, WAIT, WAIT on God. We must wait on instructions from God. DO NOT MAKE A MOVE UNTIL HE SPEAKS! Do not allow man to push you to deliver prophetic words. We sometimes can see a person's desires and we prophesy it. We must take care. This

TRAINING THE PROPHETS

may not be God's desire for them. Do not "forth-tell" this. Only say what GOD SAYS!

We must fight the urge to speak to make ourselves popular and well-known. We cannot afford to be one of those "false" prophets Ezekiel lamented for in Chapter 13 of his writings. For reasons other than godly ones, those prophets lied about the visions, dreams, and words supposedly given by God. **THIS IS A VERY DANGEROUS AND DEADLY ROAD TO TRAVEL.** Why does this tactic so anger our God? The false prophet employs the demonic spirit of seduction to lead God's people astray. If you recall, this was the same reason God <u>HATED</u> Jezebel. The spirit of influence is powerful in both the right hands as well as the wrong hands. Check yourself prophets of God. Is fame and celebrity status worth risking the wrath of God? Damaged souls are too great a price to pay.

TRAINING THE PROPHETS

The Prophet experiences the glory of God in adverse situations. John the beloved of God wrote in *Rev 1:9 "I John, who also am your brother, and companion in tribulation, and in the kingdom and patience of Jesus Christ, was in the isle that is called Patmos, for the word of God, and for the testimony of Jesus Christ."* What was Patmos? It was a small rocky island belonging to the group called the "Sporades", in that part of the Aegean known as the Icarian Sea – New Ephesus in Asia Minor. It was a place of banishment for prisoners. Each prisoner was compelled to work the mines of the islands.

Why was John there? First and foremost he was exiled by the Emperor Domitian and banished by him to this place. Next, he was chosen by God to write unhindered the profound end-time prophecy and warning signs of the coming Anti-Christ. God uses this Patmos experience as an example to prophets everywhere that God's most insightful words to you to deliver to His people are born out of extreme **personal** perilous circumstances. John's overall message was one of hope; correction; events to come; the ultimate victory of Jesus over **ALL** evil; and, warnings to the body of Christ. *Revelation 1:1-3* give us further insight to God's reason for John's residence in this lonely place.

What did John see? He was given a revelation – Greek word (apokalupsis) meaning to unveil; uncover; implies lifting the cover so all can see to share with the "body of Christ". He was given a message from Christ concerning His people, Himself, and evil. He was shown events from John's day until now that must come to pass. He was instructed to write that a blessing awaits those who read, hears, and keeps the words of this prophecy.

How did John respond to what he saw? John saw in vivid detail i.e. color, dimension, etc. The awe of the presence of God caused John to fall as dead. A fear came over him that caused God to re-assure him. John encountered the glory of God. And, you too, prophet of God, will have some of those same experiences. John has taught us how to respond. You may actually travel out of body to the very throne of God. You may interact with heavenly residents. Your brain will record vivid emotions e.g. weeping in heaven. John actually tasted the sweet/bitter book. This is a critical time. We can be so overwhelmed by the spiritual that we mistakenly try to worship angels – BE AWARE!!!

This call comes at a GREAT PRICE. God has chosen the prophet to convey his plan to mankind in a detail that he has not given anyone else. The prophet may experience times of extreme trials but there will also be times of unparalleled anointing and an experience of the glory of God in a new realm. Like all prophets, our message is that of hope, correction, coming events, warnings, and the defeat of all evil by the Omnipotence of God. God has repeatedly used the

TRAINING THE PROPHETS

prophet to unveil His divine plan. God gives the prophet a "right now" message to His people concerning the "realness and validity" of Jesus.

We will see in the spirit realm – in color and extreme detail. The presence of God will be physically overwhelming. God will reveal parts of heaven that he has not revealed to many – for us to share with others – this will bring **HOPE**! We can and will interact with heaven and visit it as well. No matter how hard the work in the mines of Patmos and the countless other atrocities encountered by John, we see this Apostle of Jesus praying for Jesus to come quickly – because he too had hope by what he had seen and heard.

Here is a question I get asked repeatedly, "Why is it that no one prophesizes to me like everyone else? God's response is "Why do you need a third party? I speak to you MYSELF." Much of what you need to know, God will tell you or inform you through your Mentor (see the chapter on "The Prophet as Student"). Why are we seeking for a "word" anyway? Stop trying to fit in.

A Prophet finds favor with God and man. Samuel had it *(1 Samuel 2:26)*. Jesus had it *(Luke 2:52)*. The apostles had it *(Acts 2:47)*. What is this favor? It is a countenance that accompanies one that is completely obedient and yielded to God. Men want to bless you. The peace and love of God are your traveling companions. This creates an atmosphere that others want to engage in – want to be a part of. God's face is shining upon you and it is visible for all to witness. So Prophet of God –walk in favor - that is – walk in integrity, honor and purity.

TRAINING THE PROPHETS

What's on my heart: Fasting and praying is the Prophet's most fundamental weapon of warfare. The worst attacks we will ever encounter from the enemy will be in the area of PRIDE and FEAR. Look at Elijah in the cave hiding from Jezebel and supposing himself to be the LAST prophet on earth *(1 Kings 19:9-18)*.

Look at Jonah's rebellion and anger aimed at God for His compassion in desiring to restore Nineveh (Jonah 1:1-3). Paul's initial refused John Mark because of his desertion but subsequently requested John Mark to join Paul's missionary journey *(Acts 15:34-37 & 1 Tim 4:10-12)*. Pride displayed in Peter's acts of hypocrisy *(Acts 11:6-8)*. Moses exhibited great anger with the children of God concerning water from the rock *(Num 21:10-12)*. The point being, we are not supermen and superwomen. The enemy deceives us into thinking that we are above temptation or yielding to it.

TRAINING THE PROPHETS

Do not think that you're beyond Satan's reach. Remember it is *the "little foxes that spoil the vine" (Song of Solomon 2:15).* We do not want to "spew" out words that not only DO NOT come from God; but furthermore, have roots in unresolved pain or hurt. Our mandate is to heal not destroy.

Arrogance is dangerous *(Romans 12:3 & Galatians 6:3-5).* Be true to yourself and God, always realizing that it is His power that provides you the opportunity to serve Him and mankind. **Abide in this attitude, mingled with fervent and effectual fasting and prayer, and your prophetic ministry will have the potential to soar to a height that you would never have imagined.**

TRAINING THE PROPHETS

TRAINING THE PROPHETS

CHAPTER 6 – THE PROPHET AS STUDENT

A God-sent mentor is **essential** for the development and cultivation of a "budding" prophet. All through the word of God we see this process in action; that of, seasoned prophet pouring knowledge into the apprentice. It is very important that the prophet realizes that he/she requires training from those pioneers in the call that have weathered the storms and have the battle scars to substantiate their longevity and triumphs.

Do not misinterpret the scripture found in *1 John 2:26-28*. The Holy Spirit is our teacher and will guide us into divine truth…but…everyone, with the exception of God Himself, has required teaching and training from one that came before. We are not so anointed and appointed that God is training us Himself. NO, He has engaged anointed men and women to train the prophets. We are not so special that God has deviated from His process of man-training-man to personally train us because we are so very "extraordinary" to Him. Don't allow Satan to feel your head with that garbage. You need a **MENTOR** to keep you on track so that you have some accountability for your actions. When we are novices, we have the potential to severely harm souls. John sounded the alarm that seducing spirits are out to cause the prophets to err and when we do, it has a negative ripple effect throughout the body of Christ.

Be aware that the mentor-apprentice relationship is a premeditated, two-way agreement that is confirmed by God to both parties. That union is only a blessing if it is sanctioned by the Holy Spirit. We don't just see a powerful Mentor (ministering under the anointing) and decide "I want **that** person to train me".

First, your motives are all wrong. The anointing is not a lotion that can be rubbed on those that seek Him or be obtained by being in close proximity to Him. Instead,

TRAINING THE PROPHETS

it is a very real transference of power that exists when God has put together a Mentor-Apprentice union. The most impressive example of this is the story of Elijah's whirlwind departure from this life. Elisha asked for a "double portion" of Elijah's prophetic power and received just that.

I want to bring this to your attention. The mentor should expect his apprentice to surpass him in ministry. Elisha received a double portion of Elijah's anointing. Jesus promised that we would do "greater" works than He did. The legacy that each Prophet-mentor leaves behind is wrapped up in an apprentice that excels into realms of ministry not experienced by the mentor. There is no need for jealousy from the mentor or arrogance from the apprentice regarding this phenomenon because it is God's natural order of the call. Instead of wasting time on those worthless,

TRAINING THE PROPHETS

draining emotions, devote it to enjoying the unique relationship shared by mentor and apprentice.

God will inform both parties that this is a pact predestined by Him. There will be mutual commitment to the time required to get the younger Prophet to a position of fitness for the ministry. Neither party should enter this agreement recklessly. Much prayer by both parties should accompany this assignment

Jesus understood a prophet must be trained. At an early age, He recognized the need to be taught by the "doctors" of the law and his parents as well. He submitted himself to 30 years of training as a living testament to the value of an appropriate foundation. *Luke 2:52 states "And Jesus increased in wisdom and stature, and in favor with God and man."* All this happened as a result of His submission to teaching from mere human beings. He then trained his hand-picked

TRAINING THE PROPHETS

twelve men and dispensed wisdom, knowledge, and power to them so that their prophetic journeys would flourish.

My mentor Bishop Daniel M. Jordan says "no experience is a wasted experience." This statement is so appropriate when discussing the relationship of Eli and Samuel and Saul (aka Paul) and his training by the Pharisees. Some mentors that God chooses for us are training us in reverse order. By that, I mean that their lives may not exemplify the high standard God requires but watching God's chastening, punishment, and reprimand provides the apprentice a first-hand lesson-learned seminar of "what not to do" in the prophetic call. Eli could not rule his own house and his own children. This was not an attribute that God rewarded favorably. Saul (Paul) learned the "letter" of the law but also saw the arrogant display that the Pharisees portrayed as religious leaders. Paul realized and understood our

TRAINING THE PROPHETS

modern-day cliché that education without salvation is an abomination. His teachers/mentors were versed in the law but did not apply the principals to their daily lives. A mentor is as much an example as he/she is a teacher. Both characteristics are indispensable to the development of the apprentice.

My mentors (Bishop Jordan and Pastor Irma Keith) taught me every aspect of the prophetic call you can imagine. I was trained in the operation of the gifts of the Spirit. Remember, I stated in a prior chapter that the Prophet utilizes two or more gifts at any given time in the ministry. *1 Corinthians 12:7-10* demands a more in-depth discussion. It states *"But the manifestation of the Spirit is given to every man to profit withal. For to one is given by the Spirit the word of wisdom; to another the word of knowledge by the same Spirit; To another faith by the same Spirit; to another the gifts of healing by the same Spirit; To another the working of miracles; to another prophecy; to another discerning of spirits; to another divers kinds of tongues; to another the interpretation of tongues".* A prophet MUST learn how to maneuver in the gifts; what the function of each gift satisfies; when a gift is operating; how to properly entreat the Holy Spirit as that gift is operating and when the Holy Spirit is finished with you and the gift. Satan is standing by to provoke you to continue ministering when the Holy Spirit has **cut the power** on the gift. One of the most profound lessons I have ether learned from my mentors is this – WHEN THE SPIRIT IS FINISHED, SO ARE YOU! IF YOU CONTINUE, FLESH IS IN CHARGE NOT GOD!

I was trained to recognize God's timing. The right thing at the wrong time is just as damaging as the wrong thing at the right time. Do not just hear the instructions from God but hear the **"WHEN"** of the instructions. Out-of-synch instructions can be fatal to the recipient. God is clear in what He wants. He does not have to speak in riddles or fairy tales. He furnishes the Prophet with the full scope of the assignment and wants him/her to use the entire arsenal of weapons and tools to perform our duties.

I was trained to value the <u>Community of Prophets</u>. Just as a parent teaches the siblings to live in harmony in the same house; so, the mentor trains the apprentices to "celebrate" one another. This notion of *celebrating* each other is nothing Satan enjoys. He will use every opportunity to pit one prophet against another. Petty differences can cause life-long rifts in relationships. I was vehemently trained to recognize entry of the enemy in our <u>Community of Prophets</u> and denounce him immediately before he could build a stronghold. I was taught to appreciate the distinct differences in other prophets because God designed us this way to reach across the globe.

TRAINING THE PROPHETS

The gift of discernment was a key topic of research. A learned mentor equips the apprentice with knowledge regarding the development of discernment. He/she teaches the apprentice how to recognize and engage demonic powers; what duties are assigned to demon powers; the atmosphere that demons cannot remain in (i.e. praise, worship and reverence to God); and, how to be victorious over demons. A learned mentor teaches how to recognize and entreat angels; atmosphere that invites the glory of God; and, what duties are assigned to angels. After all, discernment is the gift of recognition – spiritual powers in play – good or evil – holy or unholy. As a prophet, you will be destroyed if you do not develop this gift to its fullest.

I'm pausing here to address the Mentor. Hebrews 5:11-6:1 makes a perfect point that needs to be

TRAINING THE PROPHETS

addressed to the mentors. Seniority in the call does not equate to knowledge or skill. The writer was concerned that those who teach may actually be in need of teaching themselves. What is this attraction to wanting to be someone's mentor? Do we think that this relationship will validate our ministries? Are we looking for a fan club or to be viewed as one on a higher spiritual level than most? Weakness begets weakness. If you are not mentor material – please stay out of that arena. I know this sounds harsh and it is harsh but I have seen too many folks shipwrecked because they had formed an alliance with a mentor that did not know much more than they did and more importantly, did not acknowledge or recognize their deficiencies. **THIS IS SO, SO, DETRIMENTAL.** Please heed what I am saying here. PLEASE!

TRAINING THE PROPHETS

The bible is an excellent source of stories about inspiring mentors and talented student as well. Joshua took the reins from Moses and did what Moses could not do – lead the nation of Israel into the Promised Land. Elisha did twice as many miracles as his mentor Elijah. John the Divine visited heaven and wrote the most compelling account of the events of the end time, yet his past testimony was that he deserted our Lord Jesus Christ. Peter, a patriarch of renown, denied Christ three times. Paul persecuted the church unmercifully but became one of the starches supporters of the teachings of Christ. Dear Timothy, under Paul's guidance, became one of the youngest elders in the New Testament church. There is no limit to what God will do through you when you submit yourself to godly supervision, counseling, and training from a Mentor.

TRAINING THE PROPHETS

♡ **What's on my heart:** It is an honor to mentor a prophet in the making. Do not try to make "carbon-copies" of yourself in the mentoring process. God made each person unique. His purpose dictates that individual differences are key elements to reaching all people everywhere. Do not think of yourself as so evolved that a mentor is not needed. Under certain circumstances, double portions are only transferred between mentor and apprentice. Enjoy the beautiful exchange in the mentor-apprentice relationship. You will find this to be a time of much spiritual awakening in the utilization of the gifts of the Spirit and in the clarity of your hearing from God.

TRAINING THE PROPHETS

CHAPTER 7 - THE PROPHET AND THE SUPERNATURAL

The prophet does more than "speak" for God. He is God's hand of power. Remember, at any given time, the prophet engages two or more of the nine (supernatural) gifts of the Spirit to perform his/her duties as prescribed by the Holy Spirit.

The "supernatural" is a phenomenon that many people don't fully understand. The very word "supernatural" implies something beyond natural, something beyond this visible world, something that transcends the laws of nature. The supernatural is a very REAL world that is rarely seen by the human eye and operates outside of the realm of the five-senses (i.e. taste, touch, feel, smell, and hearing). God and His angels as well as Satan and his imps reside in this realm called the supernatural. Only with the assistance of our

TRAINING THE PROPHETS

Lord and His heavenly army can the prophet successfully engage in war in the supernatural arena against Satan and his demonic militia. The war must be fought with spiritual weaponry guided by divine orders from our Lord (read 2 Corinthians 10:4).

Let's look more in depth at the relationship the prophet has with the supernatural world. In *John 2:1-11*, Jesus turns water into wine, His first miracle. Those around you may recognize the supernatural anointing in you before you do – just as Jesus' mother did before Jesus recognized it. Prophets must be aware that there is a component of the ministry in which miracles, the supernatural, signs, and wonders are required. The timing of this phase of ministry is totally orchestrated by God, but the occasion will surface and we must be ready to step into that realm. God will let you feel and know that the season is approaching just as Jesus knew that it was not yet His time but that it was "nigh" him i.e. close at hand.

Only you can step into that realm and you alone – not your mentor or fellow prophets. Prepare yourself for this elevation by being aware of what God is doing "expressly" in you. Understand and allow God to submerge you into the supernatural at even seemingly "unorthodox" occasions. Did Jesus have any idea that His first miracle would take place at a wedding? The boy scouts have a motto – "BE PREPARED". Bishop T.D. Jakes has a saying he has made famous and that is GET READY – GET READY – GET READY. God is telling us today that He can present an opportunity for the supernatural at any time. Be ye also ready!

Just as Jesus' mother expected Him to do **something** supernatural when the occasion arose, so also will those around you, dear Prophet of God, expect you to allow the supernatural to flow through you when that need arises.

Sometimes, the only answer is a supernatural one and you the prophet hold that answer. Do not push this off on anyone else. It is for you to do it and for you to usher in the supernatural answers at the appointed time. I am speaking of more than the *Mark 16:15-18* anointing promised to believers. Yes, it is the greater works spoken of by Jesus and written by *John in 14:12.*

If you look at the events of *Matthew Chapter 4* (when Jesus was led of the Spirit to be tempted in the wilderness), *John chapter 1,* and the latter part of *Matthew 4,* you will see that the wedding of Cana was after the temptation and after Jesus had called his first disciple. This lets us know that extreme Satanic activity will precede this advent of the anointing into the supernatural. Look at your life and the events of the recent past. Have you had an attack from the enemy unlike any other? Be honest! Has Satan attacked your fasting? Has Satan attacked you by tempting you to tempt God (*Matthew 4:6-7*) in some way – be honest. Has Satan tempted you with pride and glory seeking because of the anointing that you possess?

Just as Satan tried to stop Jesus from getting to the level of the supernatural by tempting Him before Jesus performed His first miracle, Satan also wants to stop you from getting there as well. No matter how hard the fight has been of late – you made it to this day, this hour! We have all possibly been operating in a "realm" of the supernatural but **NOW** a complete submersion will take place. This is the appointed time for it to happen. Look at *John 2:11 "This beginning of miracles did Jesus in Cana of Galilee, and manifested forth his glory; and his disciples believed on him."* This will be the "coming out party". This will be the equipping for the prophetic office, that is, the next dimension of anointing and service to mankind.

This will be the events that "convince" people that you are indeed an Old Testament and a New Testament prophet – of no less status than that of Isaiah, Daniel, etc. This event will be the undeniable evidence that God has chosen and anointed you an "end-time" prophet. All other roads in your ministerial life have lead to this day – *Psalm 75:1-10*.

Why the supernatural – *2 Tim 3:1-9* tells us of the kinds of spirits that will inhabit mankind – spirits that can only be defeated by the "greater works" anointing. *2 Peter 3:3* speaks of another deadly spirit – scoffers – walking after their own lusts. Scoffers are mockers – meaning to treat with ridicule, contempt, to mimic, imitate, counterfeit, express scorn, and pretenders. This can perhaps be the most dangerous and the most effective tool that Satan can deploy. He will try to make you doubt yourself, your call, your anointing, and your ability. He will try to make others doubt you and then try to mimic or counterfeit the anointing to prove that there is nothing to it. Anyone can do it – there is nothing special about it at all. Do you see why elevation into the supernatural anointing is necessary for you **RIGHT NOW!**

It is a time for supernatural hearing and supernatural word. There are two kinds of supernatural hearing. The first is the hearing that each believer has from the Holy Spirit for personal direction. For example – go here; don't go there; take this job; do not take that one – all for our personal spiritual growth.

God has chosen the prophet to have that additional kind of supernatural hearing – that of hearing instructions, directions, guidance for others. God teaches the prophet how to discern our own instructions from those instructions meant for others.

TRAINING THE PROPHETS

Along with that "training" comes the understanding of how powerful and supernatural our words are – WE SPEAK FOR GOD. NOT UNLIKE THE PRESIDENT'S CABINET SPEAKS FOR HIM.

In *Matthew 8:8*, we see the power of the prophet's word. He needs simply to speak the word only because he has the supernatural, God's Omnipotent power at his disposal. In *Ezekiel 37*, God instructs the prophet to prophesy to the dry bones and it will live again.

The prophet administers supernatural healing by THE WORD that is spoken in the stead of God. The word God sends comes in many forms. One of His most powerful methods is to use the prophet to convey his message of deliverance. The power of the word the prophet speaks ALONE is enough to heal, deliver, recover, restore and revive the people of God. We prophesy to the dry bones of mankind – those steeped deep in sin – we prophesy a message of life and our words will breathe "new" life into them.

What is so supernatural about the words the prophet speaks? It is stated in the second half of *2 Chronicles 20:20 "...Hear me, O Judah, and ye inhabitants of Jerusalem; Believe in the LORD your God, so shall ye be established; believe his prophets, so shall ye prosper."* Proverbs 18:21 has already stated how powerful the tongue can be – having the power to give life or take it. *Hebrews 4:12* paints a clear picture of how deep the word of God (from God) can penetrate all the way into the inner recesses of the heart. It is the God-breathed word. It is a healing word. It is a life-changing word.

The prophet is that "mouth". He is sent to convey God's thought and ways because God's thoughts are foreign to mortal man. The prophet comes to dispel all the lies that Satan has used to beguile the people.

TRAINING THE PROPHETS

Instead, the prophet has come to inform the people that Jesus is a friend to all sinners. The prophet conveys, in God's own words, God's true feeling about mankind – his compassion, and the ultimate sacrifice made for him.

The bible is full of numerous examples of the supernatural ministry of the prophet. Review these occurrences in scripture in which Elijah is our guide and teacher: drought (*1Kings 17:1; James 5:17*); meal and oil multiplied (*1 Kings 17:14*); child restored to life (*1 Kings 17:22*); and the sacrifice consumed by fire *(1 Kings 18:38)*

Elisha's historically account is that he did twice as many miracles as his mentor (Elijah). Here is his supernatural resume: Jordan River divided (*2 Kings 2:14*); mocking children torn by bears (*2 Kings 2:24*); Naaman miraculously healed of an incurable disease *(2 Kings 5:10)*; a child raised from death to life (*2 Kings 4:35*).

TRAINING THE PROPHETS

Finally, let's look at the Prophet's encounter with the enemy face-to-face. Elisha (*2 Kings 6:8-23*) confronts the enemy with faith, without fear, and with the confidence that comes from seeing with a spiritual eye the legion of warring angels assigned to assist him. Suppose you were in the place of Elijah (*1 Kings 18:21-40*) and had to face-off against 450 of Baal's prophets. What a contest to see which power would win, that of the prophet or of the idol worshipping astrologers and soothsayers. God's prophet triumphs in every challenge because he has mastered the art of using the supernatural power invested in him by God to defeat Satan each and every time.

♡ What's on my heart. *Proverbs 14:12* informs us that every person must know that the prophetic word is not just *a word* but a SUPERNATURAL word. The prophet's understanding of the power in his/her words is the first submersion into the supernatural realm. All miracles and signs flow from that understanding. To recap, remember that the fundamental structure of the ministry of the prophet lies in utilizing the nine gifts of the Spirit i.e. word of wisdom; word of knowledge; faith; healing; working of miracles; prophecy; discerning of spirits; divers kinds of tongues; interpretation of tongues. Also remember that at any given time several of these gifts are in operation. These gifts are the portal into the supernatural world and also the basis of the prophet's continual victory over Satanic powers. Now that we have the 66 books of the bible as our manuscript **showcasing** the power available to us, each prophet should aspire to reach a higher level of that power in his/her ministry. Supernatural tools in the prophetic ministry should be common occurrences that progresses in intensity as the prophet matures in

TRAINING THE PROPHETS

his/her call. Satan has always known how potentially **devastating** the prophet **CAN BE** to his kingdom. Oh but you, prophet of God, are in a season in which YOU must not only realize this, but WALK IN IT as well.

TRAINING THE PROPHETS

TRAINING THE PROPHETS

CHAPTER 8 – HUMILITY

The word humble is defined as compliant (conforming to the desires of another), submissive (yielding your will to that of another), and subdued (taking low estate in a matter). Therefore, we can conclude that God wants us to completely yield our methods, thoughts, and actions to His plan. He orchestrates and we execute. It is His divine order of how the prophetic ministry advances.

Humility is a necessity for those called to the office of a Prophet. Just as the physical body cannot survive without water; so, the prophet **CANNOT** survive without humility. As much emphasis as possible must be brought to bear on this point because GOD WILL NOT CONTINUE TO USE A PROPHET IF HE/SHE DOES NOT POSSESS A HUMBLE SPIRIT. Humility cannot be contrived or simulated. The humble prophet will excel in the call – the arrogant prophet will soon come to ruin.

One of the best examples of a humble man is Moses. From our first encounter with Moses in *Exodus 2:10*, throughout the history of his life, we see the emergence of a profile in humility. Unlike any of us, he did not think himself adequate to take God's word to Pharaoh, Egypt, or the nation of Israel. However, one of the most marvelous of qualities we find in Moses is that he NEVER did develop an arrogant Spirit. Though God used him mightily, he stayed humble, a vessel that God could continue to use for some 40 years.

Moses never had "false" humility. He never secretly craved the praises of men while portraying to the public a different persona. No, Moses genuinely gave God credit for everything He did. What an invaluable lesson for the <u>Community of Prophets</u> to learn. I am captivated by the fact that Moses authored the first five books of the bible (The Pentateuch), wrote of himself as being the most meek man on earth *(Numbers 11:3)*, and never gives the reader the impression that he is "bragging" on himself. He recounts his acts in those books as purely informational and there is not a hint of pride as he wrote about himself in any of his writings.

Satan has tried with some success to destroy the modern-day prophet with the spirit of pride. *Proverbs 6:17* testifies that God hates pride. The Amplified Translation provides a crystal clear rendition of that scripture saying *"A proud look [__the spirit that makes one overestimate himself and underestimate others}.__"* So, Satan has used that tactic repeatedly on Prophets – promote their ministry by diminishing another prophet's ministry. GOD FORBID!

God is the power source. Ego must always be harnessed so not to eclipse the brilliance of the real

TRAINING THE PROPHETS

"Light", Our Lord Jesus Christ. *1 Peter 5:6* commands us to humble ourselves before God and in His appointed season, He will exalt us. Why are we on this constant journey to exalt ourselves?

Let's look at Moses again. God did not view him as fit to serve until he was 80 years old. How many of us will wait 80 years for our prophetic ministry to launch? Even at the end of his ministry at 120 years old, when God informed him that he would not enter the Promised Land, we do not find an account in scripture that suggest that Moses was angered by God's decision. He could have pleaded his case to God, how he faithful served Him and delivered the children of Israel out of the hand of Pharaoh or how he lead the millions of idolatrous people while many times beseeching God for mercy toward them. Yet, Moses willingly accepted the plan of God. This is the evidence God presents to us to prove that Moses indeed was one of the meekest men to walk the earth.

So, dear prophets of God, remember it is God's ministry. It is God's words. We do not **"own"** the words but are just the instruments used to release the word. When God gives a word to a prophet we should not take offense when another prophet speaks that word as their own. This is arrogance and pride. The word getting to the intended audience is the main point. Who cares where the credit goes. God should get the glory no matter what…right?

♡ <u>**What's on my heart**</u>. In conclusion, heed *Proverbs 16:*18 "Pride goeth before destruction, and an haughty spirit before a fall." Dr. Jacquie Hadnot (a wonderful prophet of God) has stated that God has

TRAINING THE PROPHETS

pulled her coattail and said "I smell pride." She immediately got on her face in repentance and supplication. Don't let God "smell" pride on you. Do not let Satan or people trick you into thinking that "you have arrived." In this desperate hour, we need all of the true prophets of God speaking the heart of God to this dying world. Stay humble so that God can **CONTINUE** to use you.

TRAINING THE PROPHETS

CHAPTER 9 – SAMUEL'S POSTURE

Posture means position, stance, or attitude; however, I would like to add a more potent description and that is **"way of life"** or **"lifestyle"** because it is imperative that the prophet strives to attain "Samuel's Posture." *1 Samuel 3:19* declares *"And Samuel grew, and the LORD was with him, and did let none of his words fall to the ground."* How was that possible? Samuel was a mere human being – just flesh and blood subject to failure and mistakes.

I am convinced that Samuel emulated the Enoch Principle. I have not heard a more eloquent or profound description than the one provided by Apostle Jerome Nelson (Spirit of Life Ministries – Houston, TX). Apostle Nelson first provides us with a Greek translation of walk [continually conversant], that is to say in constant communication with God. He goes on to say that

TRAINING THE PROPHETS

Enoch's walk with God transformed him into more of the character of God – so much so that he did not merely die but was "taken" by God. God saw a complete reflection of Himself in Enoch.

Dear Samuel had that same testimony. He was in constant communication with God. Over time, Samuel's thoughts became God's thoughts. Samuel's words metamorphosed into God's words; thus, God **DOES** not lie; therefore Samuel **DID** not lie and his words never fell to the ground. This also speaks of extreme obedience which over time is not thought of as obedience – a conscious effort to do what God asks of you. Instead, it becomes like breathing or eating - effortless and without thought – it becomes you.

I must state this as well. I envision Samuel to be a very healthy individual. Why? Think about it. When God's complete desire for you becomes like "skin" to you, that is, so much a part of you as your natural skin, then

TRAINING THE PROPHETS

we eat, wear, rest, do whatever God says. God's desires become our desires in EVERY area of our lives. If we are in the Samuel posture, we are completely fit in ALL area of our lives, completely balanced because God is a balanced God.

I am captivated by *1 Samuel 9:15-19.* Let's examine it. *"Now the LORD had told Samuel in his ear a day before Saul came, saying, Tomorrow about this time I will send thee a man out of the land of Benjamin, and thou shalt anoint him to be captain over my people Israel, that he may save my people out of the hand of the Philistines: for I have looked upon my people, because their cry is come unto me. And when Samuel saw Saul, the LORD said unto him, Behold the man whom I spake to thee of! This same shall reign over my people. Then Saul drew near to Samuel in the gate, and said, Tell me, I pray thee, where the seer's house is. And Samuel answered Saul, and said, I am the seer: go up before me* unto the high place; for ye shall eat with me today, and tomorrow I will let thee go, and will tell thee all that is in thine heart."* This is an aspect of the "posture" that all prophets should make every effort to acquire. God speaking into the "ear" of Samuel and then Samuel having the ability to tell Saul "all that is in thine heart" implies an intimacy with God that can only be that of the Enoch phenomenon.

There is very little written in the Holy Scriptures regarding Enoch but the few references that are noted in Genesis and Hebrews is so compelling that all who read it find themselves vehemently trying to achieve that same testimony. *Genesis 5:21-24* states *(Amplified Version) "When Jared was 162 years old, he became the father of Enoch. After the birth of Enoch, Jared lived another 800 years, and he had other sons and daughters. Jared lived 962 years, and then he died. When Enoch was 65 years old, he became the father of Methuselah.*

TRAINING THE PROPHETS

After the birth of Methuselah, Enoch lived in close fellowship with God for another 300 years, and he had other sons and daughters. Enoch lived 365 years, walking in close fellowship with God. Then one day he disappeared, because God took him. Hebrews 11:5 says of Enoch *"It was by faith that Enoch was taken up to heaven without dying—he disappeared, because God took him. For before he was taken up, he was known as a person who pleased God."*

We can deduce from these few scriptures that God wanted us to know about the longevity of the relationship He and Enoch shared – some 300 years. What a powerful legacy to leave for posterity, to have walked with God relentlessly for all that time. He was so loved by God that he just disappeared and did not, at that time, taste death.

The point I am making is that Samuel **HAD** to have that same Enoch testimony because the Holy Spirit

TRAINING THE PROPHETS

dictated to the writer of *1 Samuel Chapter 3* that Samuel was a Prophet whose words were always confirmed by God and would always be truth. Samuel has such power with God that God would reveal to Samuel **EVERYTHING** that was in the heart of Saul. I don't know about you but I am committing my life to obtaining that kind of power with God. We see the process for accomplishing this. We simply need to "walk with God all the days of our lives" following the pattern set forth by Samuel and Enoch. Yes it will take volumes of fasting, praying and staying before God, but Prophets of God, it is worth it. I have kicked mediocrity to the curb and want all that God has for me. What about you? Would you like the testimony that none of your words fell to the ground; that you could expose all that is in the heart of a man/woman? **DO NOT SETTLE FOR ANYTHING LESS!**

TRAINING THE PROPHETS

CHAPTER 10 - SUMMARY

It has been a joy writing this book. The many revelations I received from the Holy Spirit have been regurgitated in this manuscript. My desire is that those who read this book will find assistance in "moving" in the prophetic realm; satisfaction and comfort in their calling; and, insight in how to confidently, efficiently and successfully be used by God in this end-time.

My conclusion will center on the importance of the prophet possessing the fruit of the spirit. *(Gal 5:22-23) "But the fruit of the Spirit is love, joy, peace, longsuffering, gentleness, goodness, faith, Meekness, temperance: against such there is no law."* I know that you have heard and taught on this subject many times; but, please allow me to share my insight on the magnitude of influence the fruit will have on your ministry.

TRAINING THE PROPHETS

LOVE. We all know that love is the most powerful force on earth and that man has been commanded by God to love Him and one another. A prophet must possess <u>without measure</u> that "agape" love God talked about. Why is it so imperative that the end-time prophet have this kind of love? First, the bible informs us that the "love of many shall wax cold". We will encounter many cold-hearted, conscious-less folks. It is only through the "agape" love for the soul (that resides within those individuals) that will defeat the spirit of discouragement and the spirit of weariness-in-well-doing sent on assignment to the Prophets by Satan. Secondarily, the prophet will see evil personified, deeds done in the flesh of unimaginable proportions. He/she must see beyond the fault and recognize the great need required by man in this most critical time. Yes, souls are at stake and the prophet plays an essential role in the rescue of those souls from the grips of the enemy. So, love the man but hate the sin and tell him/her what "*thus saith the Lord*".

JOY. We have quoted the "*the joy of the Lord is your strength" (Nehemiah 8:10)*, so much that we are callous to its importance and effect. With the state of our society in much disarray, maintaining our joy is more than a "good" thing to do; it is a survival tool. Satan's device is to make the prophet so full of concern (I call it worry), so distracted by issues with our health, so depleted of our natural and spiritual strength, that we are not much use to God. At any and all costs, the prophet must retain the zeal for the ministry God has called him/her to. What actually is the "joy of the Lord"? I believe it to be a **supernatural energy intertwined with a made-up mind that will face head-on the attacks from the enemy.** Satan will attack your integrity, having the question "Are you a false prophet" noised about. Satan will attack your finances. He will attack your body and he will attack your mind. Satan ultimately wants to stop you from speaking forth the desires of the Father. Your only defense is to have complete confidence and _**gladness**_ in the One who called you and in your knowing that you are the ESTHER (symbolically speaking) called for such a time as this. Dear prophet, the day is far spent and the enemy has his "last days" power surge. If ever mankind needed you, he needs you more now than at any other era of history. So, stay focused and keep your joy. Pray in the Holy Ghost! Read books that produce life! Sing songs of deliverance! Encourage yourself and other prophets!

PEACE. Jesus exclaimed in *John 14:27* that he was leaving behind a peace very different than the kind the world was accustomed to or even knew about. Everyone is looking for peace. They may not use that exact word for it; but, nonetheless, they are searching for peace. Why is peace so vital to the Prophet? The end-times are full of turmoil and confusion. The prophet is the voice of order and clarity. If Satan can destroy the peace (harmony, order, and accord) in the prophet's life, the "hearing of God" is negatively affected. If Satan can get us to buy-into the madness around us, and get caught up in the latest crisis of the hour, how can the prophet adequately perform his/her duties as prescribed by the Holy Spirit? The peace that Jesus left for us is described in *Philippians 4:7* as one that surpasses all our understanding. What a powerful instrument of ministry at our disposal to be able to assist the Sprit in imparting peace into lives of those tormented by the enemy. <u>So, guard your peace.</u> Do not allow anyone or any circumstance to disturb the peace of God that secures your access to the supernatural realm so that you may assist others in their quest for freedom from the grips of the enemy.

TRAINING THE PROPHETS

LONGSUFFERING. This fruit has few friends. Who really wants to patiently endure lasting offense or hardship (Merriam-Webster)? The answer is NOBODY. We have been conditioned *not* to pray for patience. Some bible translations have patience as the fruit of the Spirit instead of longsuffering. You, prophet of God, will need patience to wait on God to speak. You will need patience to wait on your calling. You will need patience to perfect your calling. You will need patience with God's people. **You just need patience!** You will need patience to go through the "molding" process. You will need patience to endure the aloneness, uncertainty, and difficulties associated with obeying God in this prophetic walk. **Again, I say, you just need patience!** Accept and embrace patience. Satan is always in a hurry, but you dear prophet need not be. Stay calm and wait on God. Do not allow the enemy to PUSH you into any situation that God did not ordain.

TRAINING THE PROPHETS

GENTLENESS. Prophets can be so matter-of-fact, that they appear to be harsh and cold. Our Lord told us to be wise as serpents but gentle as doves. Jesus did not advocate weakness in any form. He does, however, want us to be gentle with God's creation – mankind. What is gentleness? It is tenderness, tranquility, and sympathy (Webster's Thesaurus). The prophet is the voice of God i.e. he is the calming agent when the storms are raging. He speaks for God to defuse the chaos of the world. To do that, the prophet must dwell in a spirit of gentleness. We are, after all, ambassadors of Jesus Christ. Gentleness is not a character flaw. Instead, it is a supernatural strength that marries tenderness with the delivery of the "cold hard facts". How many times have we heard "it is not what you say but how you say it"? A spirit of gentleness will soothe and comfort the two-edged sword rebuke that the Prophet must dispense from time to time. Pray to be gentle. So many people have been lost to the world because the words from the Prophet were so uncaring and brutal. We want to destroy sin without killing the spirit. Don't we?

GOODNESS. The *Psalmist* wrote in *23:6* that goodness and mercy shall follow us all the days of our lives. God is good and the response is ….all the time. If that is so, then we (Prophets of the Most High) are to be good! Goodness is also pure, righteous, honorable, unspotted, profitable, useful, valuable, etc. Do you see why we must possess and walk in this fruit? What use is a prophet to God when goodness is lacking? Goodness will draw people into repentance and open the door for God's forgiveness. Goodness is remembered and celebrated. *Ps 31:19* tells us that God's goodness is a reward for them that fear and trust in Him. I cannot emphasize enough the legacy that a life of goodness will produce. The prophet's words will be remembered when it is wrapped up in an attitude and expression of goodness. We don't need more insensitive prophets; we've got plenty of those. No, we need some honorable prophets. We need some gracious prophets. We need some prophets that are really concern about the man and not just delivering a word. In these perilous times, we need more prophets that possess the fruit of <u>GOODNESS</u>. We need to stop hurting God's people and again become what God designed us to be - <u>instruments of healing</u>.

FAITH. This fruit really speak of faithfulness, which is to stick with a thing no matter how it looks or how hard the fight? Sometimes the prophet is not faithful because he/she cannot wait for the ministry to develop within God's timetable. We want instant celebrity status. We want instant fame and fortune. Longevity is an attribute that God values. How many of us would stand and proclaim the same message for 100+ years like Noah. How many would get discouraged after declaring a message to nation for some 40 years like Jeremiah did and not see any positive results? God has mandated that we stay put until he says otherwise. Don't go off on another digression because you see a "new" method yielded tremendous results for another prophet. "Stick with your stick." Don't get anxious because the people don't know your name. Don't get weary in well doing because you do not see the results **YOU** expected. "Stick with your stick." Do what God has instructed YOU to do. Stay right there and do it just like God told you to do it. Be faithful to your call and in due time, and as God sees fit, He will exalt you.

MEEKNESS. I devoted an entire chapter (8) to humility because this fruit is both crucial and strategic in the life of a prophet. A prophet must be unpretentious, modest, and unassuming in their approach to the prophetic ministry. The spotlight **MUST** remain on Jesus. We can never afford to take the glory from God. The giver of the words, power, revelation, and knowledge is God. We are mere tools of God's trade. The prophetic ministry is not about money, prestige, position, or influence. **WE ARE HERE TO SERVE AND NOT BE SERVED.** Let me say that again…**WE ARE HERE TO SERVE!**

TEMPERANCE. Self-control and self-constraint is an inexhaustible subject. God expects all of the preceding fruit to sit on the foundation of balance and control. Our anointing and prophetic powers are "null and void" when done in the environment of disorder and chaos. The spirits of the prophet are subject to the prophet *(1 Corinthians 14:32)*. Nothing we have to say or do is more important than doing it at the right time. <u>*Get over yourself. You are not really all that!*</u> Do not bring a bad reflection on your ministry and God by being OUT OF ORDER. God wants the prophet to be temperate in all aspect of their lives. So, get control of your finances, your health, your children...*just say ouch*...your marriage, your thoughts, eating habits...**ouch again**....get control and balance in your life. Without balance the prophet will never advance to the dimension God predestined for him/her. I want you to advance and grow and be the end-time prophet God birthed you to be. You can do it!

I love you dear Prophets and will continue to pray that our *Community of Prophets* will reach the nations for God. **I SOLICIT YOUR PRAYERS AS I ENDEAVOR TO DO THE WILL OF GOD AND TEACH PROPHETS TO EXCEL IN THEIR CALLING.**

TRAINING THE PROPHETS

CALL TO ALL PROPHETS

It is not a new revelation if I say to you "We are in the end-times". With this fact being more real that it has ever been in history, I want to sound the trumpet that will assemble the troops for war – The prophets of God armed with a WORD from the Lord.

Isaiah 50:4-5 (NLT) – The Sovereign Lord has given me His words of wisdom, so that I know how to comfort the weary. Morning by morning He wakens me and opens my understanding to his will. The Sovereign Lord has spoken to me, and I have listened. I have not rebelled or turned away.

Prophets, you have His word in your mouth. **Cry loud and spare not.** Let's move into a new realm of the Call. We must be more than a prophetic utterance of a new house, car, or job. The Lord demands that we reveal sin and speak out against it? I know many of you have the testimony that *Isaiah* has in *50:4-5*. The weary, broken-hearted, destitute, confused, lonely, and ignorant are waiting to hear what God has to say through you – His Prophet.

I want to encourage you. I know we are among generations of "hard-hearted folk". Who needs Jesus more than they? Now is not the time to either give up or give in to failure. We are that <u>*Community of Prophets*</u> I write about in this book. We are our brothers-keeper in this prophetic call; thus, we should be aggressively concerned about one another's welfare. You are not alone in this task. We are all hearing the heartbeat of our Lord as the tension builds for his return for the bride. The bride is not ready. We need to help her prepare. We need to help her clean her ceremonial gown. Our duties are too important for any of us to compromise now.

TRAINING THE PROPHETS

Go forth and put God's house in order. Do it with discretion, humility, and wisdom. Work with and not against the Pastors, Teachers, Apostles and Evangelist. Each of us has a job to do. We are not adversaries but allies fighting the same enemy – Satan.

Self-promotion must cease. It has taken a terrible toll on God's people and caused many to fall away. With all the souls in turmoil about every aspect of their lives, this is really not the time to be a "STAR". SOULS ARE AT STAKE. Only you can examine your hands to see if the blood of the lost is dripping from it.

I know that you face all kinds of opposition. Who better to understand what you are battling than another Prophet. Do not crawl under a rock and die. We need you desperately now. Do not allow Satan to steal your joy and take the word of God right out of your mouth. FIGHT BACK WITH EVERYTHING YOU HAVE. I have felt you in the Spirit and know that it has been difficult.

TRAINING THE PROPHETS

There is hope for you and help for you. I am throwing out a lifeline to you. You know some Prophets...call him...call her. They want to assist you in your time of need.

The kingdom suffers violence. Satan is opposing us. Our flesh is opposing us. People are opposing us. We must take this violently. This is a serious matter and it is a never-ending fight. We must be desperate to OBEY THE VOICE OF GOD!

There is still so much more to know about God and the work he has in YOU!!!

WE MUST BE VIOLENT ABOUT THE WORK OF THE LORD AND NOT ALLOW ANYONE OR ANYTHING TO STOP US!

I'M SOUNDING THE ALARM. ARISE VOICE OF GOD. ARISE!

TRAINING THE PROPHETS

PRAYER OF SALVATION – IT'S YOUR CHOICE

Perhaps you are reading this book and have not accepted Jesus the Christ as your Lord and Savior? I did and it was the best decision of my life. Soon after heeding the call from the Lord to "*come unto Him*", I began to hear his voice and understand that He was calling me into the prophetic ministry.

The bible promises *"That if thou shalt confess with thy mouth the Lord Jesus, and shalt believe in thine heart that God hath raised him from the dead, thou shalt be saved." (Romans 10:9)*

It really is very simple. Pray this prayer from your heart and receive Jesus right where you are.

"Dear Jesus, I believe that you died for me and that you rose again on the third day. I confess with my mouth that I am a sinner. I need Your love and Your forgiveness. Come into my heart and forgive me of all

my sins. I receive Your peace, joy and transforming love. Amen!"

Now dear one, get you a good bible. Allow the Lord to lead you to a place of worship where you can work out your own soul salvation and God's predestined plan for your life. Be faithful to prayer and personal time with the Lord. Obey and accept the teaching from the Pastor that God leads you to and GROW IN GRACE! My prayers are with you. Feel free to email me. drmcw52@sbcglobal.net

WELCOME TO THE FAMILY!

AUTHOR'S BIOGRAPHY

I have accepted a 3-fold call from God – that of **Prophet, Teacher, Scribe (author).** In this critical hour, I am ONE of the voices God is using to deliver the "words" from His heart to mankind. This is an assignment for life and it is my joy to fulfill it. I am sent to minister healing, truth, and deliverance to God's creation (men, women, boys, and girls); to dispel the lies perpetrated by our only enemy (Satan); to hear clearly and precisely what the Spirit of the Lord will reveal to me; and, to articulate those instructions to the body of Christ. I am a Bond-slave to Jesus Christ and have been sent to serve as His Spirit mandates.

I am a wife and mother of five children (one deceased). I gladly accept the role of grandmother to 12 wonderful and unique human beings. My love for the senior community has forged in me an advocate's attitude, and I provide a voice for them whenever the need arises. I refused to refer to our youth as Generation X/Y and chose to call them our legacy and inheritance. I believe in our youth and will use all my energy to impart into them all the revelation knowledge God has given me. I believe in them.

I am an Ordained Elder. My husband is Senior Pastor of Christ Is The Answer Ministries and I serve as Co-Pastor. We are overseers of a wonderful Covenant of Pastors in Be Thou Encouraged Ministries.

Pursuing an education has been a lifelong journey. My formal education includes a BA in Psychology, Masters in Pastoral Theology, and Doctorate in Counseling. Counseling is one of my passions and I am an advocate for those hurting and in need. Faith Bible College (Independence, MO) is a superior institution of higher learning and it was my pleasure to have been one of its professors for more than eleven years.

Serving in the kingdom has been crucial to my spiritual development. God has allowed me to gain experience in leading the Missionary Department, as well as, securing my Evangelist license.

<u>I LOVE GOD!</u> I am mandated, (by Him), to administer to everyone (everywhere) healing utilizing the principles of holy living, and scriptural counseling techniques. Researching, studying, and teaching God's Word is another delight. A large part of the God's ministry through me is that of <u>encouraging</u> the people of God. I dabble in poetry, am an avid writer/scribe, tutor Math, tutor Reading, train in computer skills, conduct seminars, and facilitate conferences.

MY TESTIMONY...
On December 31, 1989, I died in the church. I had no pulse, no heart beat, nothing. My spirit began to float to the ceiling of the church and I observed the events to revive me. I continued to

hover in the ceiling watching the prayers of the saints and my children crying hysterically because their Mom was dead. My pastor (of that time) Bishop Daniel M. Jordan was praying the prayer of faith and rebuking death. He stopped abruptly and stated, "I hear the Spirit of God saying for us to praise Him right now." The church began to clap and praise God with shouts of Hallelujah and after a few minutes, my Spirit was reunited with my body. I shall **NEVER** forget that day. If I were to tell you one of the greatest after-effects of that <u>out-of-body experience,</u> it would be that God put an unusual love for souls in my heart. I definitely did not have that kind of love prior to that. I thank Our Lord Jesus Christ so much for His miraculous power.

TRAINING THE PROPHETS

APPENDIX A – RECOMMENDED READING LIST

Cry Aloud Spare Not
> Dr. Jacquie Hadnot
> Eagles Eye Press LLC Publishing

To Make War With the Saints
> Dr. Jacquie Hadnot
> Eagles Eye Press LLC Publishing

The Battle for the Mind
> Tim LaHaye – Author
> Fleming H. Revell Company – Publishers

The Elijah Task
> John and Paula Sandford – Author
> Charisma House (A Strang Company) – Publishers

Spiritual Warfare
> Richard Ing – Author
> Whitaker House – Publishers

TRAINING THE PROPHETS

Fasting for Spiritual Breakthrough
    Elmer L. Towns – Author

    Regal Books – Publishers

Humility
    C. Peter Wagner – Author
    Regal books – Publishers

Humility
    Andrew Murray – Author
    Whitaker House – Publishers

TRAINING THE PROPHETS

HOW TO PURCHASE PRODUCTS

www.eepkc.com

www.trainingtheprophets.com

Or write to us:

drmcw52@sbcglobal.net

Other Products

Training the Prophets Study Guide

Alongside the "Training the Prophets" book, this guide will extract from the depth of your Spirit, all that God has imparted into you to position you to be **HIS VOICE** in this critical hour.

Other Products

Teaching

CDs & DVDs

I love to teach God's Word and have a variety of subjects available to be an aid to you. May you be enlightened and encouraged as you study with me God's Holy Word.

Coming Soon

More **"Triumphant Living"** books

"Training the Prophet II"

TRAINING THE PROPHETS

www.ingramcontent.com/pod-product-compliance
Lightning Source LLC
Chambersburg PA
CBHW050638160426
43194CB00010B/1720